Steps in Home Economics
BOOK 2
Gillian Hodge

Hutchinson

London Sydney Auckland Johannesburg

Hutchinson Education

An imprint of Century Hutchinson Ltd

62-65 Chandos Place, London WC2N 4NW

Century Hutchinson Australia Pty Ltd
89-91 Albion Street, Surry Hills, New South Wales 2010, Australia

Century Hutchinson New Zealand Limited
PO Box 40-086, Glenfield, Auckland 10, New Zealand

Century Hutchinson South Africa (Pty) Ltd
PO Box 337, Bergvlei 2012, South Africa

First published 1987
Reprinted 1989

© Gillian Hodge 1987
Illustrations © Hutchinson Education 1987
Typeset in 11 on 13pt Helvetica and illustrated by Tek Art Ltd,
Croydon, Surrey.

British Library Cataloguing in Publication Data

Hodge, Gillian
  Steps in home economics.
  2
  Pupil's book
  1. Home economics
  I. Title
  640   TX167

ISBN 0 09 165831 4

Printed in Great Britain by Martin's of Berwick

Acknowledgements are due to the following for permission to
 reproduce photographs and illustrations:

British Telecom p. 86;
J. Allan Cash pp. 9, 16, 27, 28, 29, 72;
Child Abuse Programme, Cambridge;
The Electricity Council p. 90;
Mary Evans Picture Library p. 78;
Fitzwilliam Museum, Cambridge p. 62
Fox Photos Ltd p. 78;
Sally & Richard Greenhill pp. 12, 14, 16, 18, 32, 34, 44, 45, 47, 48,
78, 82, 85, 93;
Health at School p. 35;
HMSO p. 20;
Nigel Luckhurst pp. 9, 12, 14, 16, 19, 21, 24, 29, 32, 34, 43, 44, 47,
48, 50, 54, 60, 62, 63, 64, 78, 81, 85;
The Photo Source p. 34;
RSPCA p. 18;
Three Lions, New York p. 85.

The author is grateful to Paul Hollings, formerly a member of the CDT
department of Keldholme School, Middlesborough, for his help on
unit 8.

Every effort has been made to obtain permission from the relevant
copyright holders but where no reply was received we have assumed
that there was no objection to our using the material.

Contents

Unit 1   What is Home Economics?

1.1	Using resources	4
1.2	Using time	6
1.3	Using energy	8
1.4	Avoiding waste	10

Unit 2   Myself, My Family and Friends

2.1	Friends	12
2.2	Relationships: groups and teams	14
2.3	The neighbourhood: groups	16
2.4	The neighbourhood: care and support	18

Unit 3   Useful Skills

3.1	Recording information	20
3.2	Communicating	22
3.3	Researching information	24
3.4	Safety skills	26

Unit 4   Safety and Protection

4.1	Clean water	28
4.2	Clean food	30
4.3	Buying and storing food	32
4.4	A healthy environment	34

Unit 5   Food

5.1	Why do we cook food?	36
5.2	How is food cooked?	38
5.3	What makes us want to eat?	40
5.4	What happens to the food we eat?	42

Unit 6   Family Education

6.1	Learning to share: mixing with others	44
6.2	Gaining confidence: coping with fears	46
6.3	Growing up safely: playing	48
6.4	Growing up safely: people	50

Unit 7   Using Tools and Equipment

7.1	The cooker: hobs	52
7.2	The cooker: the grill	54
7.3	The cooker: the oven	56
7.4	Using the sewing machine	58

Unit 8   Design for Living

8.1	Designing for safety	60
8.2	Designing for the handicapped	62
8.3	Using colour	64
8.4	Designing to solve problems	66

Unit 9   Fibres and Fabrics

9.1	Understanding colour	68
9.2	Fabrics and colour	70
9.3	The business of dyeing	72
9.4	Creating with colour	74

Unit 10   Consumer Awareness

10.1	Looking at advertising	76
10.2	Looking at packaging	78
10.3	Shops	80
10.4	Shopping	82

Recaps 1 – 10 84

Glossary 94

What is home economics?

1.1 Using resources

The Jones family lives in number six. Mr Jones has a job. Mrs Jones has a part-time cleaning job. She spends most of her time looking after Basil and Rosemary.

Home economics is concerned with using the **resources** of **time**, **energy** and **materials**.

These are resources (things to use) that we **all** have. We use these resources in our day-to-day activities. How to use them **effectively** (well) is a **skill** we can **learn**.

These two homes are side by side on a local housing estate.

The Smith family lives in number eight. Mrs Smith works every afternoon and evening. Mr Smith is on short-time work. Their two children are the same age as Rosemary and Basil.

It just happens that each family has about the same amount of money (income) coming into the house.

Here the similarities end.

The Jones family has **regular** mealtimes when they sit down **together**.
Even though their **clothes** are not **new**, the Jones family look **clean** and **fresh**.
Even when it is nearly pay-day, the Jones' have **a little money left**.
At weekends Mr and Mrs Jones take Rosemary and Basil to the coast or to the countryside.
Every year the Jones family goes on **holiday**.

The Smith children have to make their own meals. They usually have **snacks** whilst watching TV.
The Smiths **often** have **new clothes** but they do not seem to last long. Often they are **soiled** and sometimes **torn**.
Sometimes the Smiths run **short of money** well before pay-day.
Mr Smith goes out with his friends most evenings. Mrs Smith works. The children have to **look after themselves**.
The Smiths have not had a **holiday together** for years.

◆ Does this story remind you of a family you know?
◆ How do you account for the difference in **life-styles**?
It certainly has something to do with the way both families **use their resources**.
They each decide how they will use their **time, money, energy** and **materials**.
They each choose an **order of priority** (importance) for using their resources.

Things to do

1.1 Using resources

Work in groups.

The local youth club is having a party to raise funds. Everyone who goes must wear a silly hat.
The Smiths rush out and buy two hats. They are quite expensive.
The Jones look around the house for materials to make hats. They decide to spend the evening working on the hats.

1. Imagine that your group is the Jones family. Make a 'silly' hat from the materials in your tray.

> In each tray will be:
> cardboard
> crêpe paper
> scraps of fabric
> bonded, iron-on interfacing
> glue
> sewing equipment
> mystery bag of 'decorations'

2. Organize a 'silly hat' competition. Invite a guest to judge the competition.

Further work

1. Here is some unusual head-gear. Find out who wears hats like these.

  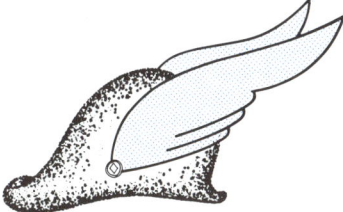

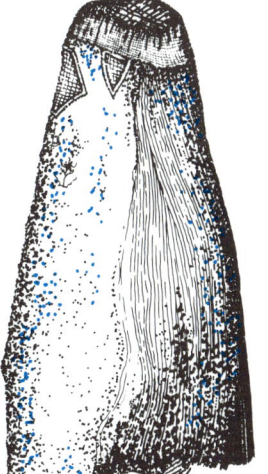

2. (a) List the resources that the Smiths used in producing their hats.
   (b) What resources did the Jones use in making their hats.
   (c) Suggest reasons for the difference in lifestyles of the two families.
4. Here is a list of activities a family might have to consider.

Providing meals	Working
Going out	Spending money
Having a holiday	on entertainment
Spending time together	Saving
Buying cigarettes	Keeping the family
Having new clothes	and home clean

List these activities in **your** order of priority.

Summary

In Home Economics we learn to make the best use of time, energy, money and materials.

What is home economics?

1.2 Using time

Have you ever realized just how many different ways we talk about **time**?
'How long does it take to cook these scones?'
'My Dad's new car can get up to 90 mph.'
'I'll see you tonight at 7.30.'
'The whistle has gone for half-time.'
'I haven't time to do anything about it now.'
'The bus takes 15 minutes to get into town.'
'I am thirteen years old today.'
In Home Economics we try to **use time effectively**. We try to get the **best value** from the **time available** to us. We **organize** or **plan** the time in which we intend to carry out a task. By careful organization and planning we make the **best use** of the time we have. We try not to **waste** time.

You have been getting up in the morning to come to school for many years now. By now you have learnt the **quickest** and **most efficient** way of using the time between waking up and arriving at school.
◆ Make a chart to show the routine you follow for getting to school in the morning.

Use a **square** for any **activity**.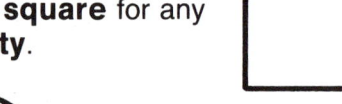

 Use a **circle** for anything that you have to **choose** or **decide**.

These **symbols** are linked by **arrows** to show the **sequence** (order) in which you do things.

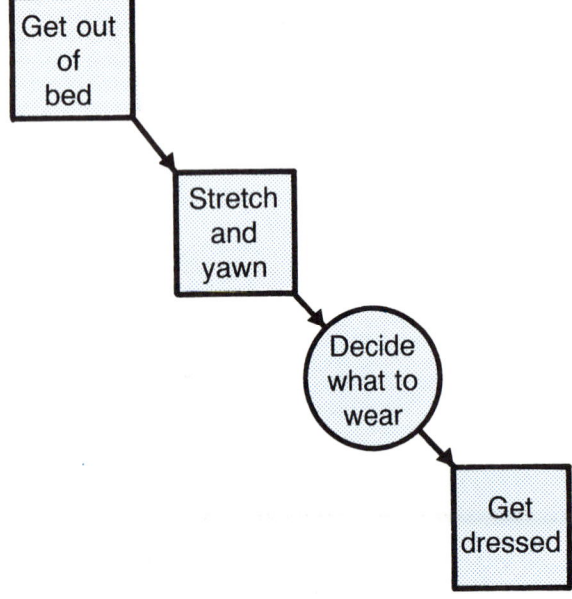

This type of chart is called a **flow-chart**.

The same routine could be written down in another way.

Time	Decision	Action
7.45		Get out of bed
7.46		Stretch and yawn
7.47	Decide what to wear	
7.50		Get dressed

This type of table is called a **time-plan**. Both methods show how we use time.

By using a **time-plan** or a **flow-chart** we can **plan ahead**. In this way we use time to the best advantage.

Things to do

1.2 Using time

You have arranged to meet a friend in the town centre at 10.20 am. You plan to choose tapes or discs and have a snack at the Burger Bar. However, your parents have one or two jobs for you to do before you leave.

Here are all the things you must do when you wake up.

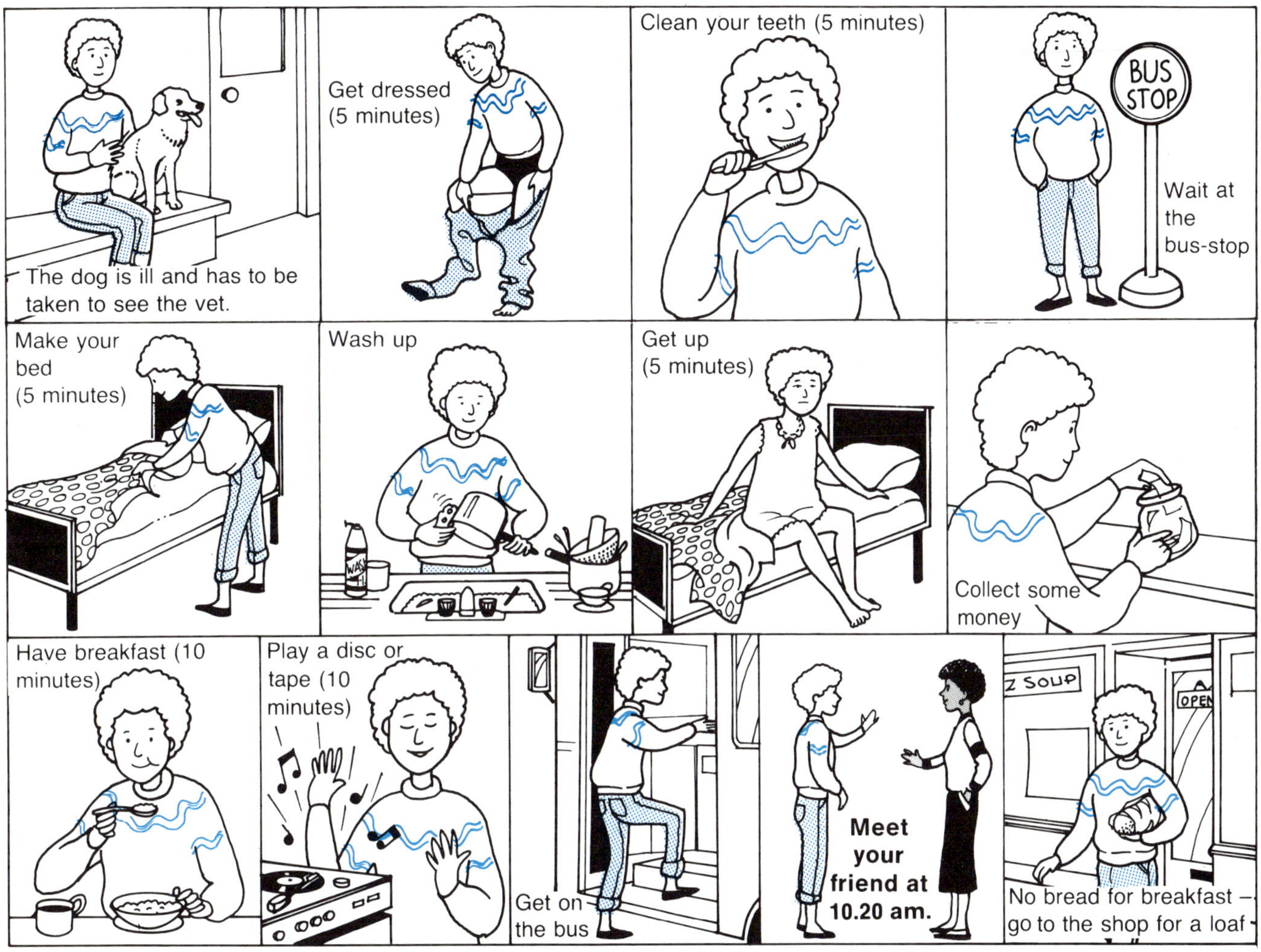

Here is some important information

1. The bus stops near your house every 15 minutes. The first bus is at 6.50 am.
2. The bus travels at 20 mph (miles per hour).
3. Your house is 3 miles from the town centre.
4. The bread shop opens at 8.30 am. It is 5 minutes walk away from your home. It takes 5 minutes to get served.
5. The vet's surgery starts at 9.30 am. The surgery is 10 minutes walk away. You have to spend 10 minutes at the surgery.

Work out either a flow-chart or a time-plan for all the things you have to do. **You must meet your friend on time**.

Further work

1. Study the sentences about time at the beginning of the previous page.
   (a) Which sentence(s) tell you about length of time?
   (b) Which sentence(s) tell you about speed?
   (c) Which sentence(s) tell you about the date?
2. Design a poster using the theme 'Time'.

In Home Economics we organize and plan time to use it most effectively.

1.3 Using energy

You know already that the **foods** you eat provide you with **energy** for **everything** you do (Book 1). This is **food energy**.

In the home, **energy** is also needed for:

Heating
Heat energy –
heats the home
heats the water and
cooks food.
It also cools the fridge
and the freezer.

Lighting
Light energy provides light wherever we need it.

Moving
Movement energy makes small appliances work.

We can choose from a variety of **fuels** to supply the **energy needs** of the home.

Coal

Gas

Oil

Electricity

The name **fossil fuels** is given to **natural gas, oil** and **coal**. This is because they are made from plants and animals that died millions of years ago. They now lie beneath the ground.

When fossil fuels are **burnt** in **air** they give **heat energy** and **light energy**. This energy can also be **harnessed** (used) to make things **move**.

Electricity is an **energy source** (not a fuel because it does not burn in air like the others).

Electrical energy can be made (generated) by burning a **fossil fuel** or from **nuclear** (atomic) power or **water** power (hydro-electric).

Fossil fuels are being used up very rapidly. They cannot be replaced.

Some people do not like the use of **atomic** power to generate electrical energy. They are looking for **alternative** sources of energy. Interest has been aroused by experiments to use:

◀ Wind power

Solar energy ▶
(from the Sun)

The power of the tides

Geothermal energy from rocks

Things to do

1.3 Using energy

Divide the class into 3 groups.

Each group will make a detailed study of **one fossil fuel**. Use the resources of the school library.

You will need to:
1. gather your information
2. research your topic
3. record your information in a variety of ways
4. present your work.

Discuss the best way to carry out this work. Use the skills of the people in your group.

A

B

C

A Coal mining, B Natural gas plant, C Oil refinery

Further work

1. Make a hot drink for a night-cap.
   List the different ways in which you use energy, from when you start to make the drink to when you put away the cup.
2. What type of energy is used when you:
   (a) make toast
   (b) have a bath
   (c) do some press-ups
   (d) use a torch
   (e) run upstairs
   (f) turn on the TV
   (g) fry an egg
   (h) use the vacuum cleaner?
3. Complete the crossword.

Clues across
- **2** Where solar energy comes from (3)
- **6** Not strictly a fuel (11)
- **9** Geothermal energy comes from these
- **10 & 11** Fossil fuels were formed from these (7) (6)
- **12** Mining this is a dangerous job (4)
- **13** A fossil fuel (9)

Clues down
- **1** Hydro-electric power comes from this (5)
- **3** Produced from the North Sea (7, 3)
- **4** GENERATOR
- **5** The ebb and flow of the sea (5)
- **7** An alternative source of energy (4)
- **8** Name given to fuels formed from dead plants and animals (6)

Summary

In the home we use heat energy, light energy and movement energy.

What is home economics?

1.4 Avoiding waste

◆ Has your family had a **new car** recently or a **washing machine**? Perhaps you are lucky enough to have a **computer** or a **cassette player**. Think about all the things you use at home which are worked by **electricity**.

Think about the ways in which we **heat** and **light** our homes and **cook** our food.

The **fossil fuels** we use **will run out**. Experts tell us that in the second decade of the next century (2010–2020 AD) most **oil** and **natural gas** will have **gone**. In about 300 years time (2300 AD) there will be little useful **coal** left.

It makes sense to use the fuels we have **carefully**. It could be **many years** before efficient **alternative** sources of energy are developed.

In the home we use all types of fuel for **heating, lighting** and **cooking**. How can we set about making sure we are not being **wasteful**? After all, it is in our own interests to be careful. We have to **pay** for the fuels we use.

Here are some ideas to get you started. Explain the statements below.

Cooking

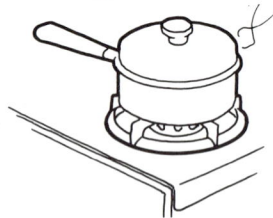
Do not allow the gas flame to come up the sides of the pan. Use a lid on the pan.

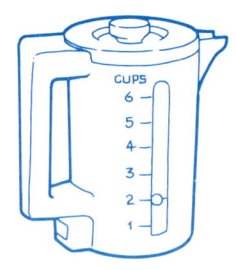
Heat only the amount of water you need.

Do not heat the oven to cook one dish only.

Why is it wasteful to put warm food in the refrigerator?

Heating water

Do not allow taps to drip, especially the hot tap.

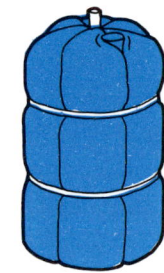
Insulate the hot water cylinder.

Why is it more economical to take a shower than a bath?

Do not wash up under a running tap. Use a washing up bowl in the sink.

Heating the home

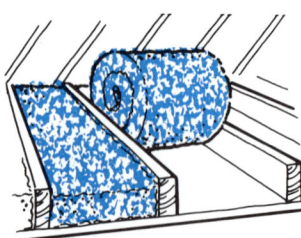
Insulate the loft.

Draw curtains at night.

Fit draught excluders to doors and windows.

Turn down room thermostats a few degrees. Wear an extra sweater.

Using lights

Use a bulb which gives enough light for the job.

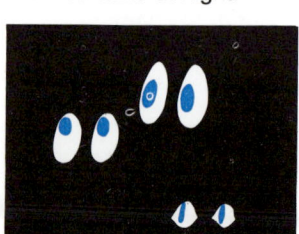
Switch off lights when you leave a room for any length of time.

When decorating, remember that colours can affect the amount of light.

Keep light fittings clean.

Things to do

1.4 Avoiding waste

Work in small groups.

Paying for gas and electricity
Gas is measured by **volume**. We buy gas by the **cubic foot**. The amount used is recorded on a **meter**. Look carefully at a gas meter.

A **digital** meter moves on **one digit** (figure) every time **100 cubic feet** of gas are used.

On a **clock meter** dials record the amount of gas used.
Read the dials starting at the bottom left. The important figure (which gives the reading) is the one the dial has just **passed**.

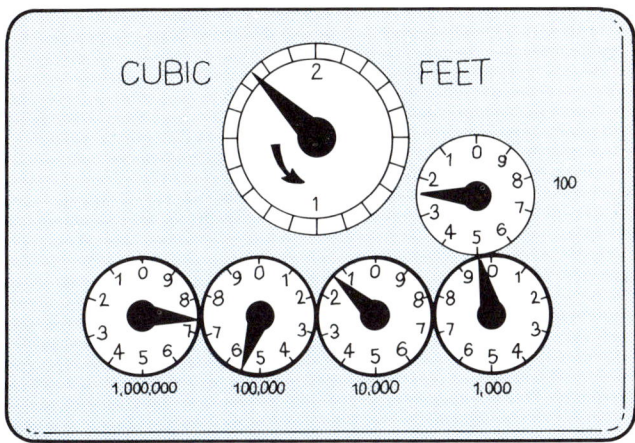

◆ Read the meter recordings above.

100 cubic feet of gas is called a therm.

The gas is charged for in **therms**.

◆ Study a gas bill. Find out the cost of a therm of gas.

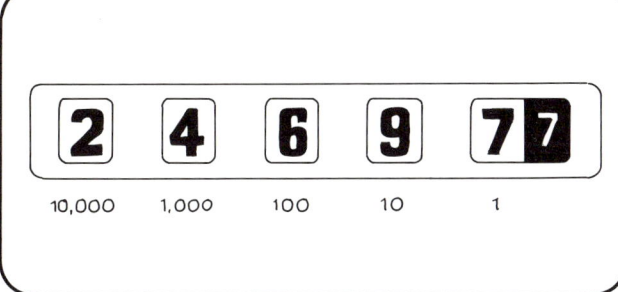

Electricity passes through the **meter** as it enters the house. The amount of electricity used is recorded in **units**. The meter might be the **digital** type or the **clock** type.

◆ Read this meter. Remember to start at the **left** and to record the figure the dial has just **passed**.

◆ Study an electricity bill. Find out the cost of one unit of electricity in your area.

1 unit of electricity represents 1000 watts (1 kW) consumed (used) in 1 hour.
If you know the **wattage** of a piece of equipment, you can work out what it costs to run.

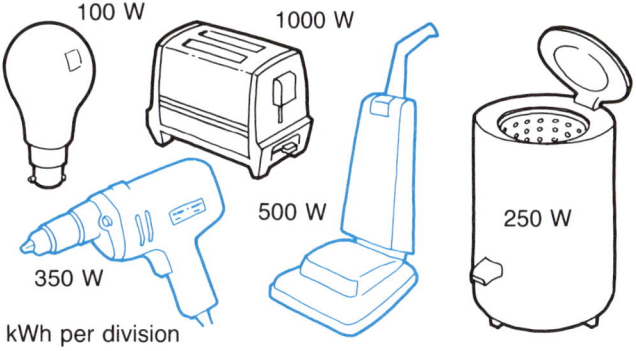

kWh per division

◆ How long will it take these appliances to consume 1 unit of electricity?

Further work

1. Make a careful drawing of either a gas or an electricity meter.
2. Explain how either gas or electricity is paid for.
3. How often do gas or electricity bills have to be paid?
4. Design a board game to be played with counters which encourages the players to save energy.

Summary

Oil and gas reserves may run out in about 35 years time at the present rate of use.
Coal seams could be exhausted in 300 years.

Myself, my family and friends

2.1 Friends

Think about the people who are your **friends**. You have probably been friends for some time. Perhaps one of your friends is **more important** to you than the others.

◆ Do you know why?
Often it is hard to know why friendship is important.

When we are **worried** or **unhappy** it helps to be able to talk about things to a **friend**.

Most of us want to have someone we can **confide** in and tell our **secrets** to.

When we are upset we want **sympathy**.

We expect our friends to be **loyal** and we **trust** them to stand by us.

Sharing **interests** and funny stories with someone who **understands** us increases our **enjoyment**.

It is important to remember that your friends **need you** for exactly the same reasons. There will be days when they are **angry, sad, jealous, worried, happy, excited** or **frightened**.
At times like these you will have to give them **consideration** and **support**.

Through friendships we learn how to get along with other people. Friendships also help us to understand our own **emotions** and how to cope with them.

Things to do

2.1 Friends

Activity 1

Study these friendship scenes and answer the questions.

A

Lisa joined the class in the second year. She was tall for her age, nice-looking and full of fun. She did well in her lessons and was good at sport.

Fay, who had been rather lonely, thought she was great fun. She became friendly with Lisa.

Fay's mother was a widow. Each afternoon she waited for Fay to get home before she went out to work.

Lisa persuaded Fay to go into town with her after school.

Questions

1. Explain what you think Fay felt when faced with this situation.
2. Why do you think Fay did what Lisa suggested?
3. What do you think Fay's mother's reaction would be?
4. What should Fay have done in a situation like this?
5. Imagine you are Lisa and try to give reasons for your actions.

B

Alan walked to school unhappily. His dog had been run over the night before and he was very worried about it. Suddenly he saw Janice. She was crying. He asked her what was wrong. Janice explained that her gran had died in hospital the previous day. She felt better when she had told Alan all about it.

Questions

1. What do you think Alan felt about his dog's accident?
2. Explain why Janice was so upset.
3. Why do you think Janice felt better after talking to Alan?
4. How do you think Alan was helped with his own problem?

Further work

1. Use drawings and make up a 'friendship' story to illustrate two of the following: loyalty, trust, jealousy, unkindness.
2. Think about people in your class. Who would you choose:
   (a) to play football or hockey with
   (b) to work hard with
   (c) to have a good laugh with
   (d) to tell your troubles to?
   Explain why. Is it always the same person?

Friendships help us to understand our own emotions.

2.2 Relationships: groups and teams

Myself, my family and friends

A young human is **dependent** upon the **adult** for a long period of time, much longer than in any other species. During this dependent period the child learns to cope with his/her **emotions** (feelings), **physical** and **intellectual** growth and **social development** (learning to get along with others).

Early learning starts in **play**. It is through play of **different kinds** that the **skills** needed to cope with life are learned.

In Book 1 you identified the groups you belonged to in school: year group, tutor group or form, a member of the school.

We need to learn skills which help us to get along with **groups** of people. We have to learn what **part** we can play in group activities.

By now some of you will have become a member of a **team**. This could be the hockey or football team or simply a group of people who work together in class, in the choir or on the litter squad.

As a **team member** you have **responsibilities**. Other members of the team will **rely** upon you. They **trust** you to do your share of the task and not to let the team down.

Knowing that you are **trusted** helps you to feel **confident** and **valued**. In your turn you have to learn to trust others.

Through team-work, skills of **communication** are increased. Team members need to be able to **communicate** their intentions **quickly** and **clearly**, by **word** or by **body language**. Because team members know each other well they develop a **sensitivity** to each other's needs and reactions.

A good team member works for the good of the team.

Things to do

2.2 Relationships: groups and teams

Activity 1

(a) Study these pictures carefully.
(b) Write a few sentences to explain what is happening.

A

Activity 2

The team selectors are choosing a new team (any sport or activity).
They ask each of you to write an advertisement describing and selling yourself as a team member.
You may use no more than **thirty** words.
Remember that you are trying to **persuade** the selectors that **you** are the person they **need**.

Put the advertisements in a hat. Take it in turns to read one. Guess who it advertises.

Further work

Look again at the pictures in A.
1. Try to explain Bob's feelings when his friend called to ask him to go to the fair.
2. How do you think the coach felt on practice night?
3. What do you think the feelings of the players were on practice night?
4. Bob does not appear to be enjoying himself at the fair. Suggest what he is thinking about.
5. Describe Bob's emotions on the day of the match.
6. What skills and qualities does a good team member need?

Summary

A good team member is loyal and reliable.

2.3 The neighbourhood: groups

Most human beings are **social** creatures. They enjoy being in groups.
◆ They are **gregarious** (seek the company of others). Why?
Throughout life **group activities** are important to them. **Skills** in relating to others are **tested** and **developed**.

Consider your own neighbourhood. You may be surprised to discover how many groups there are.

There may be groups formed by different **religious** communities in your locality.

Cultural groups exist in many large towns and cities. In these groups ex-patriots gather to maintain links with their homeland. They want to strengthen their feeling of **belonging**.

Social contact is encouraged by working men's clubs, women's organizations, parent and toddler groups, clubs for the over-sixties and many others.

Sports clubs have facilities for developing **physical skills** as well as providing a meeting place for people.

There will be branches of **national organizations** such as Girl Guides, Scouts, youth clubs, the Red Cross Society, Girls' and Boys' Brigades. The community may also have organized groups of its own; perhaps a junior jazz band or a Neighbourhood Watch scheme. Groups linked to **leisure activities** may also be represented.

Things to do

2.3 The neighbourhood: groups

Activity 1

Work in small groups.

1. Design a 'coat of arms' to represent your neighbourhood.
   The group interests and activities in your locality should be shown.
2. Mount and display your work on the classroom wall.
3. Discuss the work of each group with the rest of your class.

> You will need:
> strong paper or card
> pencils
> rubbers
> paints or coloured pencils

A

Activity 2

1. Draw a life-line (as in diagram **B**).
   1 cm represents 4 years.
2. Shade in (a) groups you have belonged to, (b) do belong to, (c) might belong to in your lifetime.
3. Use a colour code for each shaded area. Some areas may overlap.

3. Find these well known groups in this word search.

   RNLI

   NSPCC

   CUBS

   SCOUTS

   GIRL GUIDES

   RED CROSS

   SAMARITANS

   RSPCA

   OXFAM

S	C	O	U	T	S	J	M	P	G
Y	A	S	P	A	Q	B	F	B	I
M	O	M	N	I	G	F	U	V	R
O	X	F	A	M	J	U	T	C	L
L	P	B	R	R	N	A	B	M	G
I	H	D	E	S	I	K	I	A	U
L	C	Q	C	P	S	T	L	Z	I
N	S	P	C	C	H	W	A	L	D
R	O	E	X	A	K	D	Y	N	E
F	G	R	E	D	C	R	O	S	S

Further work

1. What group activities are found in the locality represented by the coat of arms in **A**?
2. Find out more about one of the groups or societies in your own area.
   This assignment could take the form of an interview:
   (a) do some background research
   (b) plan your questions
   (c) make the necessary appointments
   (d) record your work appropriately.

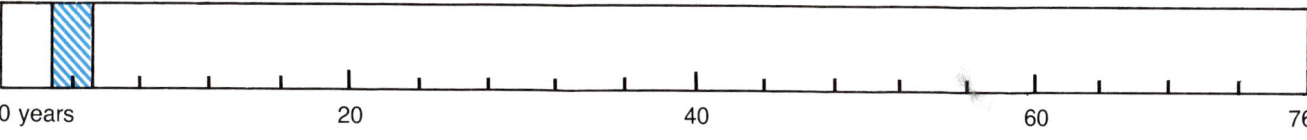

B

4. Explain what each coloured or shaded area represents. e.g.  3–5 years, pre-school playgroup.

Summary

Human beings often seek the company of others.

Myself, my family and friends

2.4 The neighbourhood: care and support

While you have been growing up someone else has taken the **responsibility** of seeing that you are well looked after.

As you grow older you have to take more responsibility for looking after yourself. You will also begin to develop a sense of **responsibility** for the **welfare** of those members of your community who are less fortunate than you.

While you are young, healthy and active you will have few problems and worries. In later life **lack of money, loneliness, ill-health, unemployment** and **old-age** can bring problems and difficulties.

The **official social services** are there to help people when times become hard. We shall consider their work in Book 3.

Often just having **someone to talk to** or knowing **where to go** for advice can help.

Many unofficial organizations play an important part in caring for and supporting members of the community.

The **Citizen's Advice Bureau** is staffed by trained volunteers. They give advice on any problem or suggest where help can be found. Throughout the country there are **Samaritan** centres. People in distress who feel they can no longer cope can contact these centres.

The **National Marriage Guidance Council** gives help to people who are having problems in their marriage.
Anyone who suspects that a child is being ill-treated or abused can contact the **NSPCC**.
The **RSPCA** will investigate cases of cruelty to or neglect of animals.

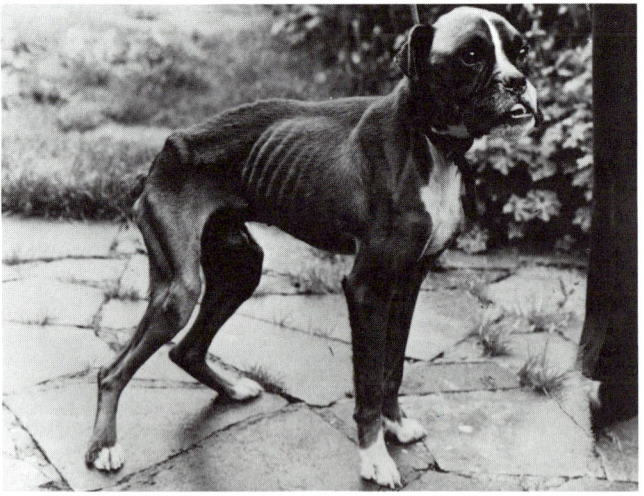

The **PDSA** centres will treat sick or injured pets.
The **Salvation Army** offers compassion and support to people who have lost all self-respect and interest in living.
The **Family Service Unit** provides accommodation for distressed families who are unable to cope. Parents are taught to use their money wisely and to run a home.

These and many other voluntary organizations rely upon the support of more fortunate members of the community.

Things to do

2.4 The neighbourhood: care and support

Activity 1

1. Study the scenes below.
2. Suggest where help can be found.

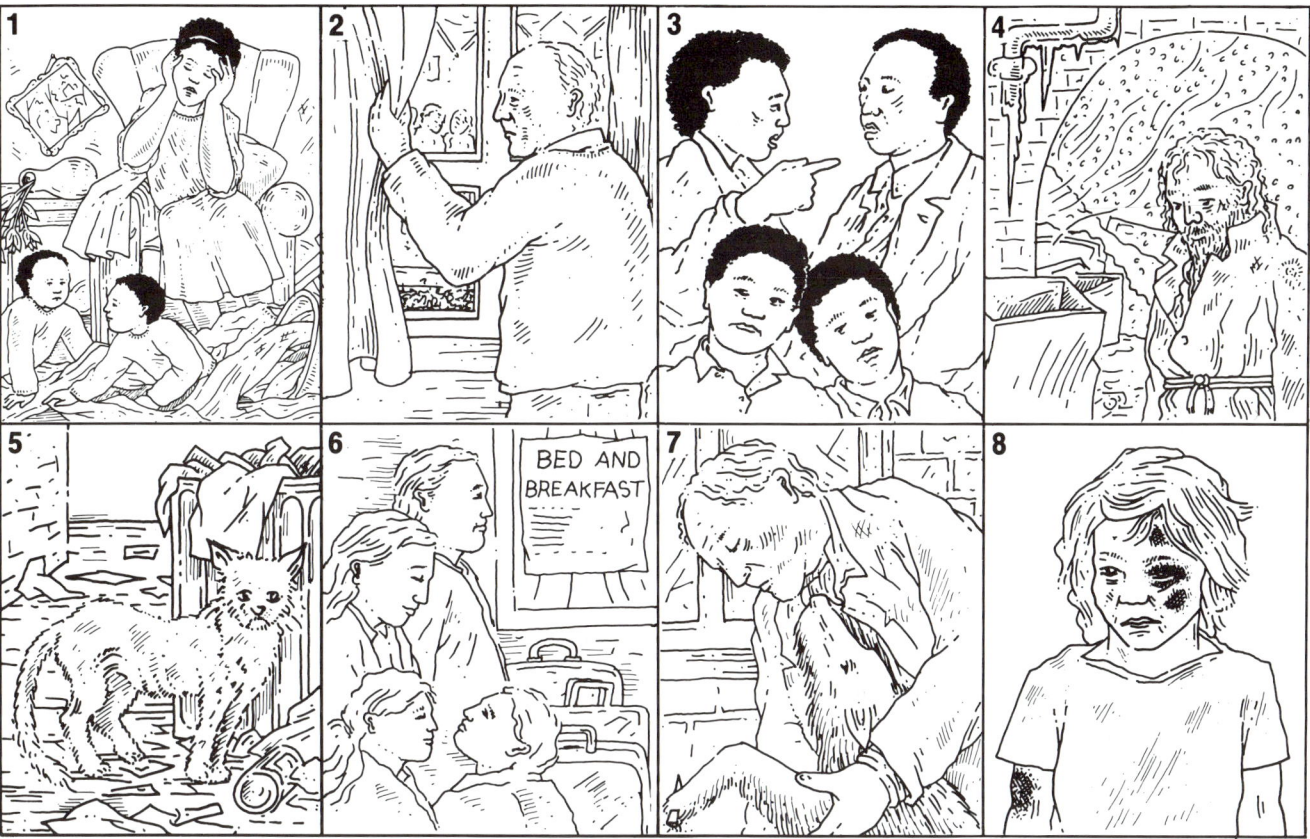

Activity 2

Working as a class or in small groups, make a gift which can be given to a local organization in the community.

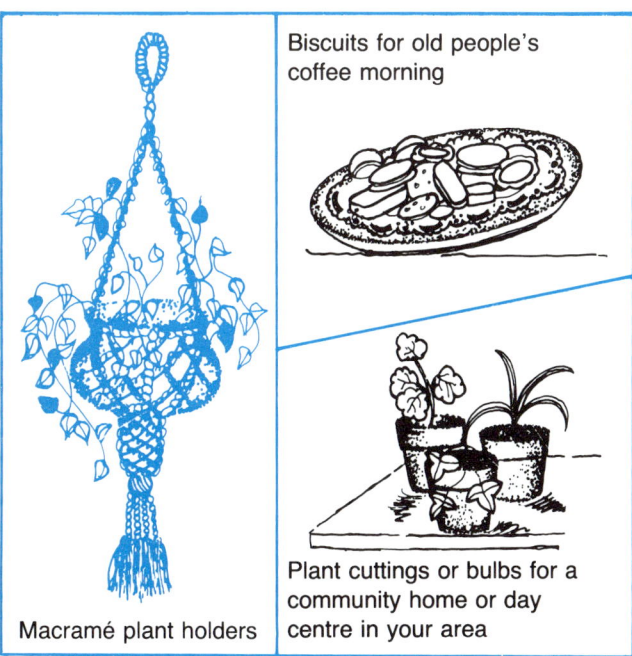

Macramé plant holders

Biscuits for old people's coffee morning

Plant cuttings or bulbs for a community home or day centre in your area

Further work

1. Find out what these abbreviations stand for: NSPCC, RSPCA, PDSA, CAB.
2. Identify this person. How does he help in the community?

3. What efforts could you make as a group which would benefit voluntary organizations?

Summary

Unofficial and voluntary groups do valuable work in the community.
They need our help and support to make their work possible.

Useful skills

3.1 Recording information

Our ancestors have left us **records** of important events as well as information about everyday living. If they had relied upon **memory**, much of what has happened would have been lost.

To be certain that you can **recall** (remember) information **accurately** it must be **recorded** with care. Making **notes** and making **sketches** are just two ways of recording information.

To become skilled at making notes you must learn to recognize **important** words or **key words**. By listing the key words you will have enough information to **remind** you about what you heard, read or saw.

◆ Look for the key words in this newspaper article.

Mr Bertie Green, a *76 year old* bachelor, had *£7400* in £5 and £10 notes in his pocket when he was found *collapsed in bed* at home at *Slough, Bucks.*, in January. *He died in hospital* two days later. Mr Charles Gray, *the coroner*, said Mr Green, a retired postal worker, *died from hypothermia* and recorded a verdict of *natural causes*.

In this passage the **key words** are about:
people – Bertie Green, coroner
places – Slough, bed, hospital
figures – 76 year old, £7400
medical information – collapsed, died, hypothermia, natural causes.

These road signs record vital information **without using words**. They use **pictures** or **symbols** to convey (pass on) their message (**pictograms**).

◆ What is the least number of words you can use to describe the hazards (dangers) shown in these symbols?

◆ Do you think words would help or hinder in getting the message across?

In Home Economics we use **graphs** to record information in a clear, concise (short) form. Graphs are used to record **observations** (**facts** or **data**) and **figures**.

By using **numbers** at the sides and by marking in (**plotting**) **data**, graphs can be drawn as **lines** or **bars**.

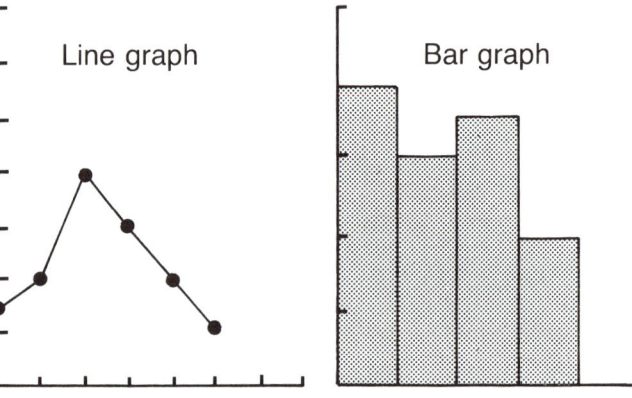

A pie graph is based on a circle.
Remember that a circle has **360°** at the centre. The **data** to be recorded are marked as **segments** (parts) of a circle.

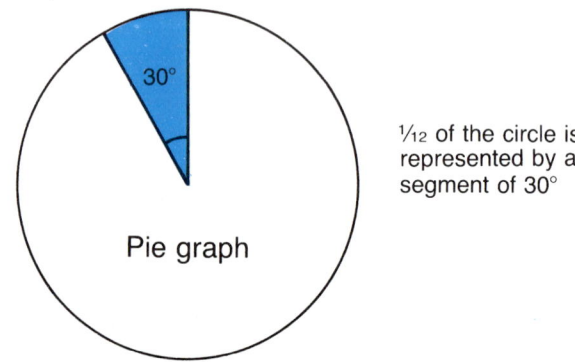

1/12 of the circle is represented by a segment of 30°

All graphs must have a title, and details of the numbers at the sides. The data must be plotted carefully and there should be a short explanation of what information the graph gives you.

Things to do

3.1 Recording information

Activity 1

Work in pairs.

1. Use a **bar graph** to record data (observations) about the colour of cars in the school car park.
   (a) Discuss how to tackle this work.
   (b) Complete the graph.

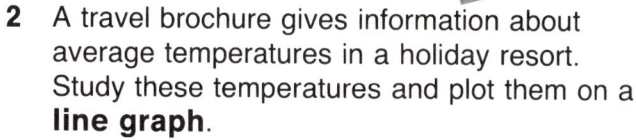

2. A travel brochure gives information about average temperatures in a holiday resort. Study these temperatures and plot them on a **line graph**.
   What does the graph show clearly that was not so obvious in the temperature table?

Temperatures in °C

January	February	March	April	May	June	July	August	September	October	November	December
16	17	19	21	22	24	25	26	24	21	20	17

3. Select twelve different items in the Home Economics room.
   Note the country of origin of each item in rough.
   Use a **pie graph** to record your data.
   In **descending** order, state the **fraction** of the total produced by each country.

Activity 2

Organize a class quiz.
Choose a person to keep the score and a person to be the reader. Divide the remainder of the class into two teams.
The reader will read out an interesting and detailed story from a newspaper or magazine. (Alternatively the teams could listen to a story cassette.)
Each team will be asked questions about **key words** in the story.
The team gaining the highest number of points for correct answers wins.

Further work

1. Listen carefully to a programme on the radio or television. Make notes of what happens using key words.
2. Today you are a newspaper reporter who has been sent to interview a politician.
   Suggest the different ways in which you could record this interview.
   Which method do you think will be most accurate? Explain why.

Summary

Recorded data and observations must be accurate.

3.2 Communicating

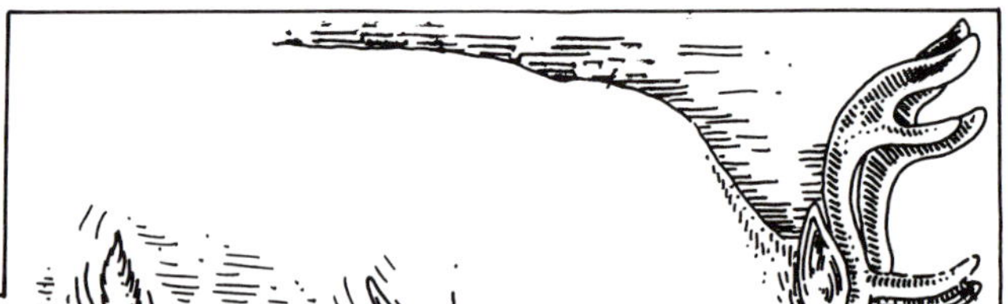

Communication is a way of passing on messages. **Animals** convey messages by sounds, scents and **behaviour patterns**. The ways in which **humans** communicate are more highly developed.

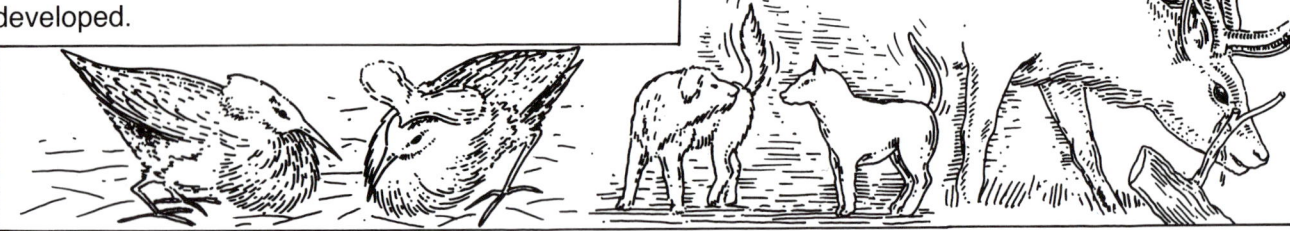

◆ Think of ways in which we let others know what we are feeling and thinking.

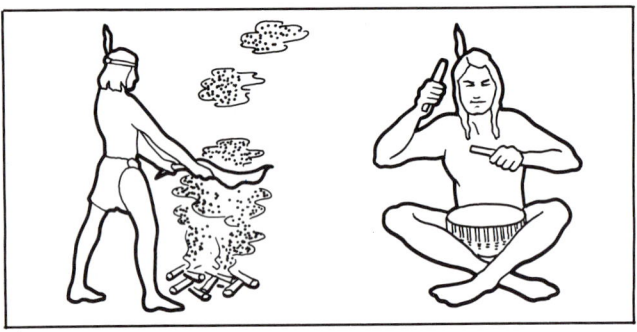

Modern technology has made communication **faster** and **easier**.

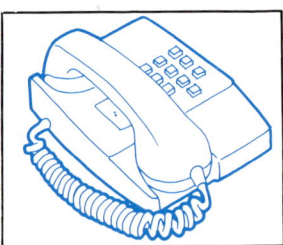

We communicate by **talking, describing** and **explaining**.
We use **telephones** to get in touch with people quickly.
We write **informal letters** to relatives and friends: thank-you letters, birthday cards and get well messages.

Flat 1b,
Seaview,
Sunsea
4.6.87

Dear Laura

You really must try to spend a few days here with us. There is such a lot to do. Not only do we swim and explore the caves but often go for walks on the cliff paths. Do try to come. Everyone hopes you are well.

With Love
from
Bob.

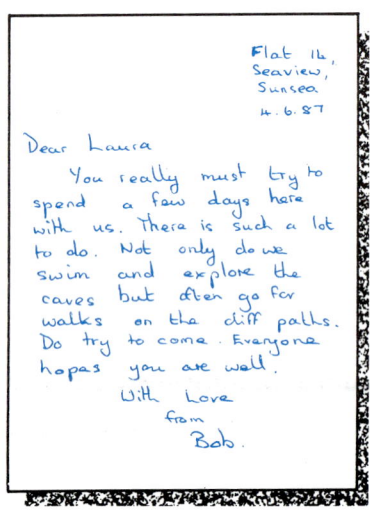

When we want to communicate with businesses we write **formal** letters.

6 Reid Street,
Baytown,
N. Yorkshire,
BT1 3AG
4.6.87

Publicity Manager,
New Theatre,
Baytown,
N. Yorkshire,
BT1 2DP

Dear Sir,

Would you please send me a copy of your forthcoming productions.
I look forward to hearing from you.

Yours faithfully,

J. Swain

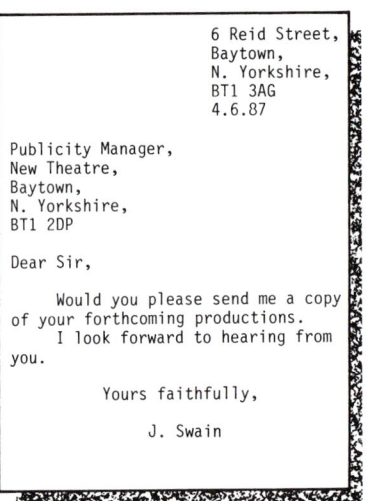

So that other people can communicate with us we need to be able to understand **graphs, charts, maps, timetables** and **diagrams** (pictograms).

We must learn to **listen** carefully for **information** and **instructions**.

In order to use goods and operate equipment safely we must be able to **read instructions**.

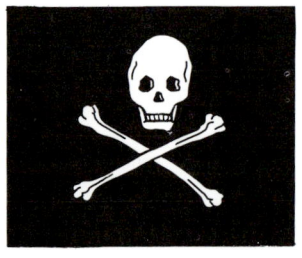

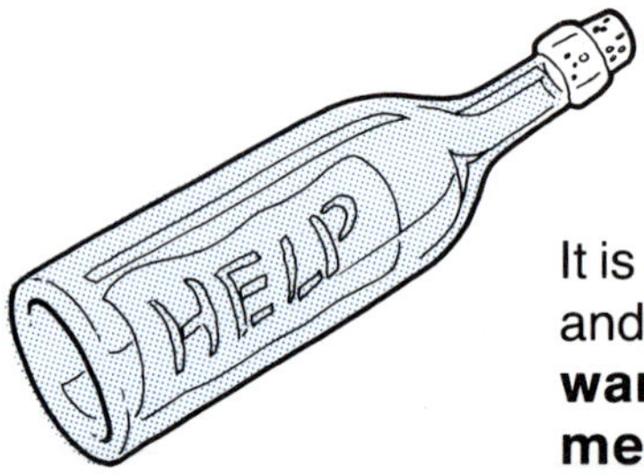

It is vital that we can read and understand **warnings** and **urgent messages**.

We need to be able to follow **verbal** and **written directions** and **give them** too.

Things to do

3.2 Communicating

Activity 1

1 Write down details of the verbal instructions you would give to a blind friend so that he/she could open a matchbox, select a match and strike it safely.

Activity 2

Study these pictures.
Picture A
1 Imagine that you are Rosemary. Write an appropriate letter to Basil.
Picture B
2 Imagine that you are Basil. Write a suitable letter to the shop manager.

Further work

1 Follow these directions to find the treasure.
  (a) From the most northerly point on the island travel 3 squares south-west and rest in a shady place.
  (b) When refreshed travel south to a dark, gloomy place where the sun does not penetrate.
  (c) Four km east and one km north you will find an islander with his home on his back. He tells you to go to the highest point on the island.
  (d) From here follow the arrow for four km.
  (e) One square south-east start to dig for treasure buried by a pirate.
  (f) Put a cross on the ground so that you know where the treasure is.
2 Design and make a get well card to give to your grandmother.

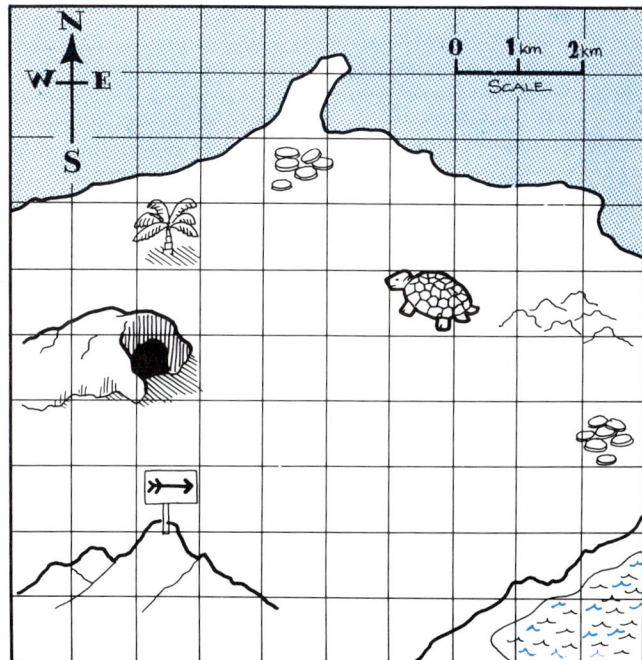

Summary

Human beings have a highly developed system of communication.

3.3 Researching information

Researching information simply means **finding out** something by **careful searching**.

No-one is expected to carry vast quantities of knowledge in his/her head. However, it is important to know **how to get at** the information you need. One of the best sources of information of all types is your **school** or **local library**.

Most libraries use the same method of organizing their book stock.
Non-fiction books are **classified** (grouped) according to their subject content (what they are about). This method of grouping is called the **Dewey Decimal Classification**. Very simply, all knowledge is divided into **ten** main classes, using the numbers 0 to 9.

000	General works
100	Philosophy
200	Religion
300	Social Sciences
400	Language
500	Pure Science
600	Technology (applied science)
700	The Arts, Recreation
800	Literature
900	History, Geography, Biography

As you can see, each **class** has **100** numbers.

Each class is then separated into **ten divisions**. E.g. Home Economics (which is in the Technology class) is covered by the numbers 640–649.

By using this system of grouping (**classification**) all information on the subject is brought together. This makes it much easier for you to find what you want.

Not all information is in book form. Maps, charts, photographs, cassettes and records can all be classified in the same way.
Use the **catalogue** in the library to find out how much and what type of information there is on the subject you want.

Books which give you information of a special kind are called **reference books**.
As these books are often large and heavy they have to remain in the library. Also, other people may want to use them too.
Once you have found the book you need, the next step is to **find the information you want** in the book.
The **quickest** way to find a particular fact is to use the **index** of the book which is usually at the back. The index is in **alphabetical order** and gives the number of the page on which the information can be found.

Index

A
Air 78
Aluminium 90
Amino acids 7, 8
Anaemia 37
Antioxidants 108
Antisplattering agents 108
Aseptic canning 101

B
Bacteria 44, 60, 94, 95-107
Baking powder 79

◆ If the book does not have an index, what other page in the book might give you a general idea of where to look for your information?

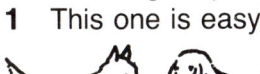
3.3 Researching information

Activity 1

a b c d e f g h i j k l m n o p q r s t u v w x y z

1 This one is easy!

Here are the names of several breeds of dog. In your book write them in a list in **alphabetical order**.

Labrador, Collie, Spaniel, Elkhound, Terrier, Husky, Rottweiler, Beagle, Doberman, Mastiff, Pointer, Whippet, Alsatian, Greyhound.

2 Now try this assortment! This time look at the **second** letter of the word.

dye desert diver dream danger door dungarees

3 Here are some names which have to be entered in the telephone directory.
When there are a lot of names the same, you should list them in the alphabetical order of their first initial first, then their second and then their third initial.

Green P.R., Green D.S.I., Green W.H., Green D.P., Green P., Green H.W., Green H.A., Green G.H., Green P.E., Green M., Green D.S.L.

Activity 2

Here is a timetable similar to the one you might find in a bus station.

Weekdays

Redgate Lane	0720	0805	1004	1147	1410	1840
Cobblers Corner	0726	0811	–	1153	1416	–
Branston Station	0745	0830	1029	1212	1435	1905
Branston Centre		0835	–	1217	1440	
Loxton		0855	–	1237	1500	

Loxton	0905	1240	1740
Branston Centre	0925	1300	1800
Branston Station	0930	1305	1805
Cobblers Corner	0949	1324	1824
Redgate Lane	0955	1330	1830

Questions

1 How long does the journey from the Redgate Lane bus-stop to Loxton take?
2 You live near Cobblers Corner. Which bus will you have to catch to be at the dentist's in Branston Centre by 1.30 pm?
3 How many buses are there each weekday which start from Redgate Lane and go all the way to Loxton?
4 A friend from Loxton is coming to visit you. You arrange to meet at Branston Station at a quarter past one in the afternoon. Which bus will your friend have to catch?
5 You have been shopping in Loxton. By 4.30 pm you are tired and decide to go home to Cobblers Corner. How long will you have to wait for the next bus home?
6 What reasons can you suggest for the bus time-table being arranged in this way?

Further work

Use your school or local library to find the answers to these questions.
1 How much blood is there in the body of an adult man?
2 Who made the first usable matches?
3 Which was the first country to use postage stamps?
4 When was the Russian Revolution?
5 What is the largest living bird?
6 How many wives did Henry VIII have?
7 List the names of Henry VIII's wives in the order in which he married them.
8 Complete these words, which are all States in the USA.

Pen . . . , Ore . . . , Miss . . . , Mont . . . , Wash . . . , Flo . . . , Ten . . . , Lou . . . , Ken . . . , Vir . . . , Wy . . . , Ari . . .

Knowing how to find out is a useful skill.

Useful skills

3.4 Safety skills

The next time you pass a building site, notice the ways in which the workers **protect** themselves from **injury**.

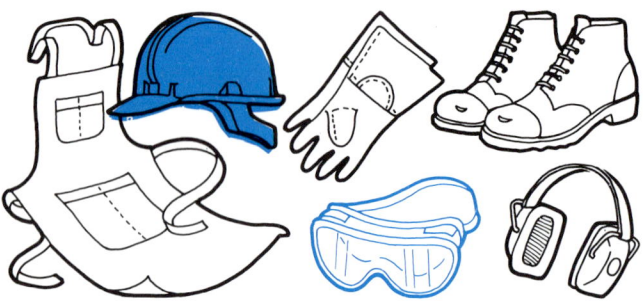

Almost every place of work has its **hazards** and employees often undergo a short period of **safety training**.

People who work in dangerous situations must learn to be aware of their **own safety** and the **safety of others**.

In school the need for safety is just as important.
You may already have discussed safe ways of using equipment and materials in the **science laboratory**, the **woodwork room**, the **metalwork shop** and others.

As a **safety precaution** in **PE** you may be asked to remove earrings, watches and other **jewellery**.
For the general safety and comfort of everyone in the school there will be **rules** affecting **movement** and **behaviour**.

◆ Find out your school's rules for clearing the building in case of fire.

◆ Look at the illustrations below. Explain the importance of these safety rules in Home Economics.

 Leave coats and bags well away from food preparation areas.

 There should be a calm atmosphere in a room where there is a lot of activity.

 Make sure you read instructions before you use goods or equipment.

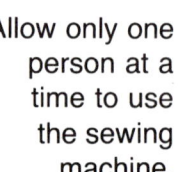
 Allow only one person at a time to use the sewing machine.

 Keep threads for hand sewing as short as possible.

 Place the ironing board alongside the wall.

 Wipe up waterspills immediately.

 Keep oven cloths and oven gloves dry.

 Handle sharp tools with care.

Things to do

3.4 Safety skills

Activity 1

Work in pairs.

Today your class is working as the **School Safety Team**. You and your partner will be **Safety Officers**.

Arrangements have been made for you to visit one of the areas in school where practical activities or movement are taking place. These places will include: games field, gymnasium, sports hall, science laboratory, woodwork room, metalwork shop, Home Economics room, school kitchen, main staircase or entrance.

Your teacher will tell you which area to visit and how long to stay there.

What to do

1. Discuss with your partner the likely hazards in your area.
2. Decide for how long you will carry out the observation.
3. Decide how you will record your data (observations).
4. Go to the area where you will carry out the task. Introduce yourselves to the teacher and explain your work.
5. Choose a sensible vantage point. Carry out your observations.
6. Report back to the rest of the class at the correct time.
7. Compile (put together) a written report to give to the person responsible for the area where the observation took place.
   Remember to make constructive (helpful) comments.

A

Further work

Safety is not something reserved just for school and work. We need to be aware of safety all the time.
Study photograph **A**.
Imagine that you are a three year old toddler shopping with one of your parents.
Describe all the dangers (hazards) which you might meet in this shopping precinct.

Summary

Become aware of safe working practices for your own sake and for the sake of others.

Safety and protection

4.1 Clean water

◆ Have you ever stopped to think just how fortunate we are to have **safe, clean** supplies of **water** to our homes?

In some countries it is **unsafe** to drink water that comes from the tap. In other countries, particularly in country areas, there is no **piped** water.

Our supply of fresh water is provided and looked after by the **regional water authority**. This service is expensive to operate and the **local authority** charges a **water rate** to every household.

◆ Where does our water come from?

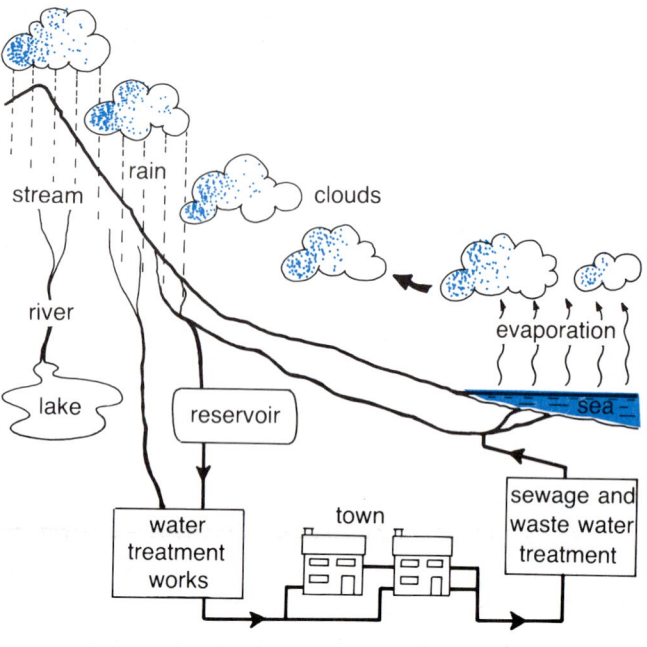

Around our land are deep seas.
The **sun** and **wind** cause some sea-water to **evaporate** and form **water vapour**.
Warmed water vapour rises. It quickly cools again as it moves away from the surface of the Earth and **condenses** into water droplets. This gives clouds.
When clouds are blown over the land, the water droplets often fall as **rain**.
The rain runs down hillsides and eventually makes small **streams**.
Small streams join up to make **lakes** and **rivers**.

Where the land is made of **permeable** rocks the water can pass through. When it reaches **impermeable** rocks or clay, the water collects to form **underground rivers** and **lakes**.

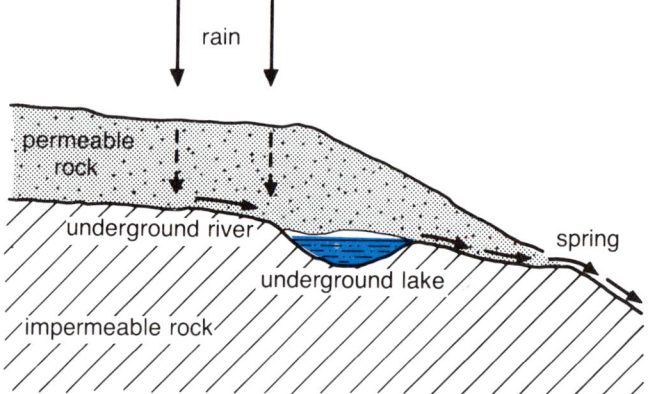

Our water supply might come from any of these sources.
Water authorities also collect water in **reservoirs**, often high up in mountains or hilly areas.

◆ Why should this water be cleaner than lowland river water?

Nowadays many people are concerned about **contamination** of river water.
Factories may discharge **waste products** into a river, killing its natural life.
Farmers use **chemicals** to fertilize the land and to get rid of pests. The chemicals can soak into the ground and find their way into streams.
Raw sewage from towns or farms can **pollute** the water.

It is the job of the regional water authority to make sure that our water supplies are safe to use.
At the **treatment works** water is **filtered** to remove stones and weeds. It is then carefully treated with **chlorine** to kill any **bacteria** before being piped into our homes.

Things to do

4.1 Clean water

Activity 1

Work in small groups.

Devise (work out) a simple experiment to show that when salt water (like the sea) evaporates and then condenses (like rain), it is salt-free.
(a) Discuss the investigation with your group.
(b) Decide how to carry out the investigation.
(c) Decide how to record your work.

Activity 2

Read the information in 4.1 again.
Make a flow-chart to record the stages in the rainfall cycle.

Further work

Study the pictures **A**, **B** and **C**.
1. How would you rate the quality of water for drinking purposes from each of these sources?
   Give reasons for your answers.
2. It is proposed that, in time, water used in the home will be measured by a meter.
   Complete this table to estimate the volume of water used in a variety of household tasks.

Task	Estimated volume of water used

Flushing the lavatory uses about 10 litres of water.

Summary

In this country the regional water authorities ensure that we have a safe water supply.

Safety and protection

4.2 Clean food

From time to time newspapers carry headlines such as this. When we read them we are reminded just how important **good food hygiene** is. **Everyone** who handles or prepares food carries a **responsibility** to practise good standards of hygiene.

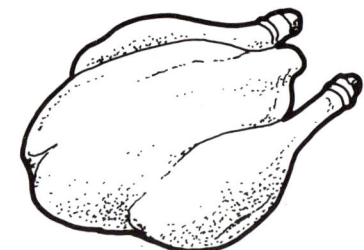

Food becomes dangerous to eat when it is **contaminated** with **micro-organisms**. Micro-organisms (such as **yeasts, moulds** and **bacteria**) are always present in the air.

Sometimes they are present in the food when we buy it. Normally the **high temperatures** used to **cook** the food **destroy** the micro-organisms and make the food safe to eat.

Places where food is **handled** and **prepared** must be **clean** and **hygienic**.
Premises where food is **cooked** for the public or **sold** to the public are checked for cleanliness and standards of hygiene by **public health inspectors**.
Your **kitchen** at home or your **Home Economics room** must be clean too. Remember to use **clean equipment, clean surfaces** and **clean cloths**.
Wash up **carefully** and wash dish cloths and tea towels **frequently**.

People who prepare food must have good standards of **personal hygiene**. That means you!

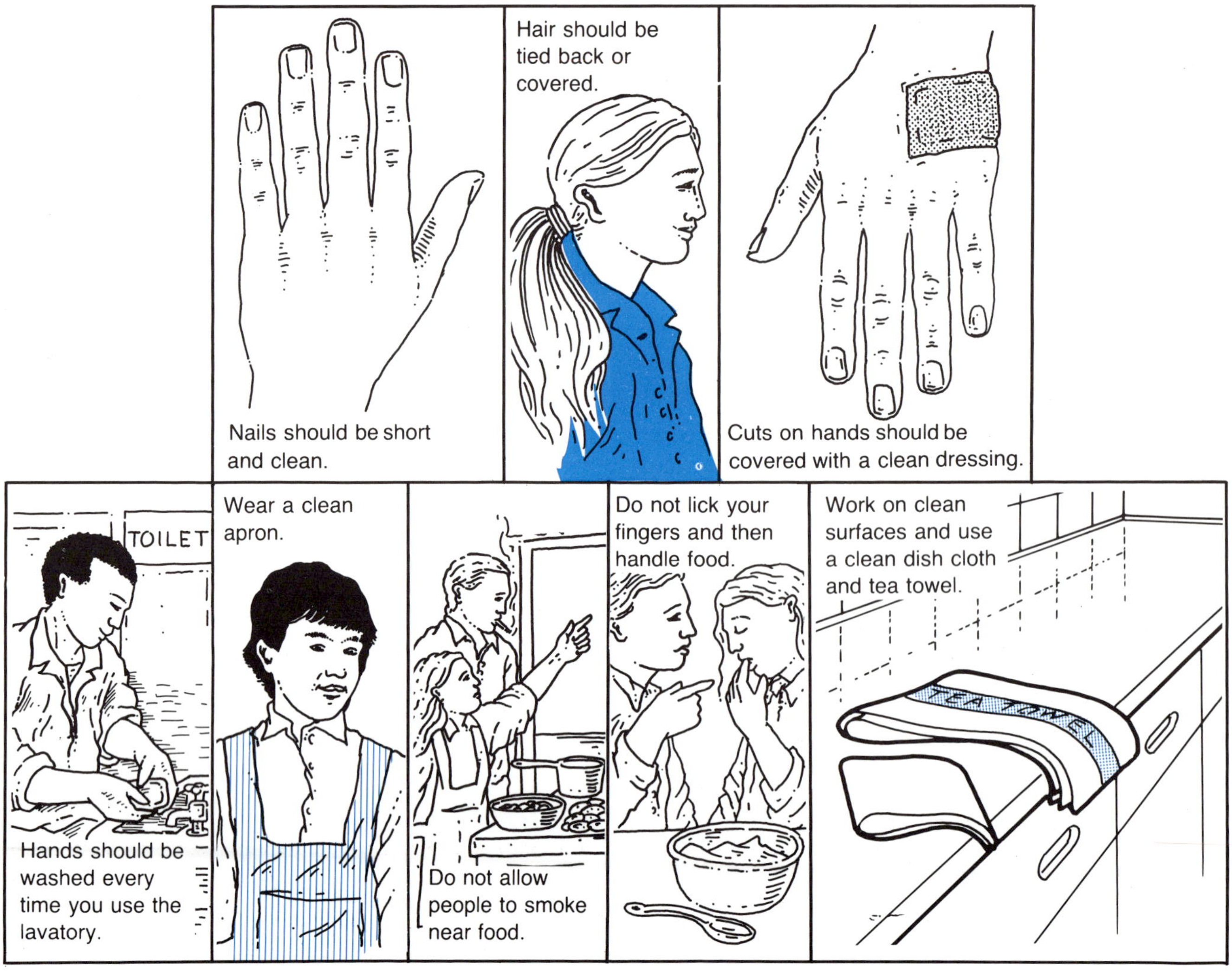

Nails should be short and clean.

Hair should be tied back or covered.

Cuts on hands should be covered with a clean dressing.

Hands should be washed every time you use the lavatory.

Wear a clean apron.

Do not allow people to smoke near food.

Do not lick your fingers and then handle food.

Work on clean surfaces and use a clean dish cloth and tea towel.

Things to do

4.2 Clean food

Activity 1

Work in groups.
Investigate the growth of micro-organisms on agar jelly.

When carrying out investigations of this ⚠ type you must obey these simple rules.

1 The investigation **must not** be carried out in a place where food is prepared.
2 Once the agar plates have been contaminated (infected) the Petri dishes must be **sealed**.
3 Once contaminated, the Petri dishes **must not be opened**.
4 When the investigation is completed the Petri dishes must be **disposed of hygienically**, preferably by burning. **Your teacher will arrange for this to be done**.
5 Wash your hands **thoroughly** after the investigation.

You will need:
6 sterilized Petri dishes
sterilized cotton wool swabs
adhesive tape
labels
agar jelly

What to do
1 Pour some agar jelly into each Petri dish until it is about half full.

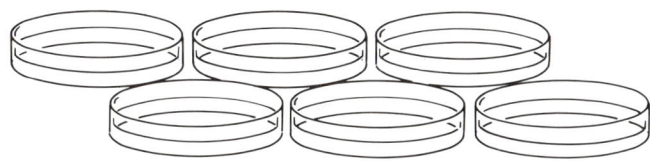

2 Cover and allow to set in the refrigerator.
3 Label one dish 'Control, refrigerator'. Seal it and place it in the fridge.

4 Label one dish 'Control, room'. Seal it and put it in a warm place in the room.
5 Label the remaining dishes a, b, c and d.
6 Use the cotton wool swabs to contaminate the agar jelly after rubbing them
 (a) on the scalp
 (b) under the fingernails
 (c) around the sink outlet
 (d) on the floor.

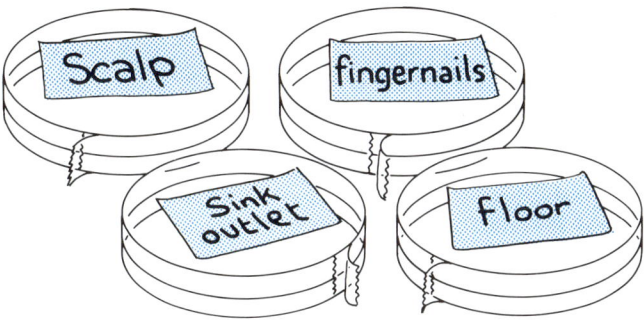

7 Cover and seal the Petri dishes. Leave them in a warm place for about **one week**.
8 Observe the Petri dishes **without opening them**.
9 Record your work in any appropriate way.

Further work

1 In Activity 1 you carried out an investigation into the growth of micro-organisms.
 (a) Explain why you had a control experiment
  (i) in the refrigerator
  (ii) in the warmth of the room.
 (b) Why did you use sterilized Petri dishes?
 (c) Why were the Petri dishes covered?
 (d) Why were you told not to work in an area where food was prepared?
 (e) Explain why the safe disposal of the Petri dishes is essential.
 (f) Under what conditions do micro-organisms thrive best?
 (g) What conditions are needed to inhibit (slow down) the growth of micro-organisms?
2 Contact your local Health Education unit for posters and information about personal hygiene. Ask permission to display the posters around the school.
3 Use your school or local library to find out the life cycle and habits of the house-fly.

Summary

Anyone who handles food must have good standards of hygiene.

Safety and protection

4.3 Buying and storing food

A careful look at the food displays in a reputable supermarket will give you an idea of the conditions under which foodstuffs should be stored. Use this information to store foods in a similar way in your own home.

Whoever does the shopping in your family should make sure that the shops they use are **clean, reputable** and have **efficient rotation of stock**.

◆ How can you tell which shops have good standards?

Assistants should never **touch open food** with their hands.

◆ Suggest ways in which direct contact with food can be reduced.

Animals should not be allowed into food shops. Animals can spread disease.

◆ What exceptions might be made?

Stocks of **fruits** and **vegetables** should be of **good quality**. Wilted and tired-looking goods should be removed regularly.

Cooked meat counters should be completely **separate** from those which deal with **raw meats**. This helps to prevent contamination.

The **overalls** the assistants wear should be **clean** and fresh looking.
Hair should be **tied back** or **covered**.

Foods which are nearing the end of their **shelf-life** should be removed when the **sell-by** date expires (runs out).

Shop assistants should not be allowed to **smoke**. Customers should also be discouraged from smoking.

Scraps of food should not be allowed to collect on counters and floors. They will attract **flies** and **vermin**.

Things to do

4.3 Buying and storing food

Activity 1

◆ Would you use this café?

List as many reasons as you can why this café could be an unhealthy place in which to eat.

Activity 2

Carry out a survey of hygiene standards in your local shops.

Name of shop	Type of shop	Hygiene practices	Rating			
			Good	Average	Below average	Poor
	Supermarket	Foods beyond sell-by date still on shelves				
	Supermarket	Clean, freshly laundered overalls				

(a) Discuss how you will carry out the survey. Think about:
  (i) the shops you will look at
  (ii) how you will operate – spot-checks or with the manager's permission
  (iii) group sizes
  (iv) which hygiene practices you will check.
  (v) how you will record your work.
(b) Carry out your survey.
(c) Discuss your results with the rest of the class.

Further work

1 Find out what happens to foods under different storage conditions.

You will need:
2 small potatoes
2 carrots
2 small pieces of cheese
2 small pieces of bread
plastic film

What to do
(a) Leave one potato in a light, sunny place. Put the other potato in a cool, dry, dark place.
(b) Leave one carrot in the warmth of the kitchen. Put the other carrot in a cool, dry, dark place.
(c) Wrap each piece of cheese in plastic film. Place one piece in the refrigerator, leave the other piece in a warm, moist place.
(d) Put one piece of bread in a cool, dry place. Put the second piece of bread in a warm, moist place.
(e) Leave for several days, then examine each foodstuff.
(f) Record your observations.
(g) Suggest suitable places and conditions for storing each of these foods.

2 To whom would you make a complaint about low standards of hygiene in a food shop?

Summary

Shop where food is stored, prepared and served in hygienic conditions.

Safety and protection

4.4 A healthy environment

Why, in our advanced society, do so many people die from illnesses linked to an unhealthy environment?

What is a **healthy** environment?

We know already how important a **varied diet, good personal hygiene, clean clothing** and **surroundings** are.
We know also that **clean food and water** are necessary for the health of people in the community.

How certain are we that the **air** we breathe is **clean** and **unpolluted**?
Polluted air contains harmful substances which can affect **health, buildings** and **animal and plant life**.
Pollution is caused by **chemical substances, smoke, dust and exhaust fumes**.

◆ What other pollutants can you think of?

Nowadays most people know that smoking **cigarettes** can damage health. How many of them realize or care that when they pollute their own environment they could also be affecting the health of others?

◆ Do you think of **noise** as a pollutant?

People who live close to busy **airports** have to live with the inescapable noise of low-flying aircraft. High levels of noise can be very distressing as well as causing **damage to hearing**. Young people who listen regularly to high volume music run a real risk of some degree of **deafness**.

People who **work** in **noisy** surroundings **protect** their hearing with **ear-muffs**.

◆ Try to think of other forms of noise which could cause stress.

People are less likely to suffer stress when they live in clean, cared-for surroundings. Where there is a sense of **community** they feel **valued** and **needed**.

It is essential that the homes of the **elderly** and **very young** are **warm** enough. In severe weather low temperatures can put the lives of old people at risk. It is not uncommon for old people to die from **hypothermia**.

As our society becomes **richer** people are getting less **exercise**.

◆ Can you suggest reasons for this?

Lack of exercise can be linked with **heart disease**, particularly when a person is **overweight, careless about diet** or is **a smoker**.

Building up and keeping a **positive attitude** to health is also important. People need to have **interests**, a **job** to go to and a **healthy environment** to work in, facilities for **exercise** and **relaxation** and **sufficient sleep**.

Things to do

4.4 A healthy environment

It is well worth remembering that what may be a **tolerable** level of sound to one person, could well be **unpleasant** noise to someone else.

Noise is a combination (mixture) of **intensity** (strength) of sound and **frequency** (pitch). **Noise levels** are recorded in units called **decibels** (dB).
Some typical noise levels are shown opposite.

Activity 1

Work as a class.

Use a noise level meter to record decibel (dB) ratings in a variety of situations in and near school:

1. woodwork room
2. metalwork room
3. library
4. dining hall
5. beside a busy road ⚠
6. at a disco.

Record your information in any suitable way.

For information

The human ear should never be exposed to *sudden* noises of more than 135 dB without ear protection.
A worker in a noisy factory must have ear protection if the *constant* noise is 90 dB or above.

Further work

Investigate the effect of smoking on the heart rate.

You will need:
watch or clock
graph paper
a relative or neighbour who smokes

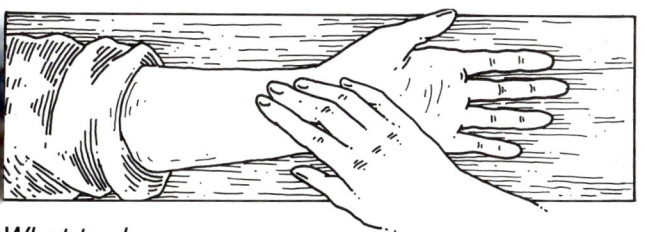

What to do

1. Place the arm of the smoker as in the diagram.
2. Place the first three fingers of your right hand on the thumb side of the smoker's upturned wrist.

decibels

Each graduation of 10 increases the intensity of sound **ten-fold**.

3. Count the number of beats felt in one minute. Take the pulse two or three times to get the average pulse rate.
4. Ask the smoker to light a cigarette. Take the pulse after three or four puffs.
5. Ask the smoker to finish smoking the cigarette. Take the pulse again.
   Take the pulse every 15 minutes until it has returned to normal.
6. Record your results on a graph.
7. Describe the effect of smoking on the heart rate.

Summary

Having a healthy environment involves us in choices.

Food

5.1 Why do we cook food?

During the **warmer weather** most of us eat **raw** vegetables in salads. We enjoy the **fresh fruits** that are in **season**.

Raw foods also form part of our diet during the **winter** months.

However, a **hot** meal on a **cold** day is most welcome. This is only **one** of the reasons for cooking food.

We cook food to **improve its flavour**. Although some foods taste good when raw, others improve with cooking.

◆ Can you think of one?

Food which has been cooked is often **easier to eat** and **digest**. Careful cooking makes the food **tender**.

The **appearance** of food is frequently improved by cooking. Making food look attractive takes skill and care.

Being able to cook food gives us the opportunity to have **variety** in our diet.

Cooking is a highly developed art. Just think of all the ways in which we use eggs or potatoes.

Some **raw** foods contain **natural poisons** (toxins). These toxins can only be destroyed by cooking, e.g. in red kidney beans.

Some raw foods **discolour** when they are exposed to the **air**. This discolouration is the result of the action of **enzymes** (chemicals which make reactions happen faster) present in the food.

◆ Think of some examples.

Sometimes food is cooked to **preserve** it. Summer fruits are boiled with sugar to make jam. Jam will keep for many months.

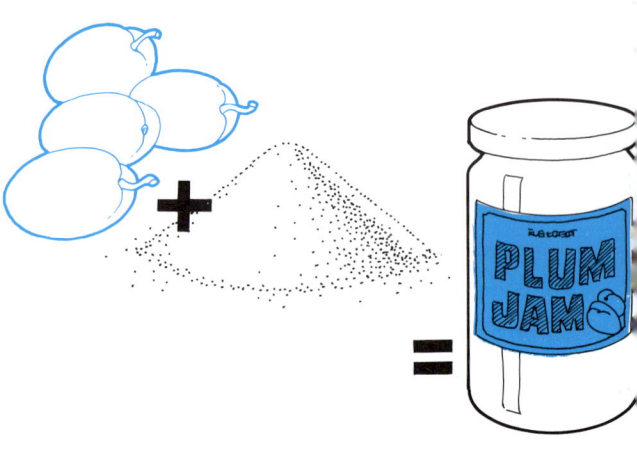

◆ Can you think of other examples?

Certain foods are attacked by **micro-organisms** yeasts, moulds and bacteria, which are present in the air. These **perishable foods** must be cooked quickly before they become inedible.

Have you ever noticed when cooking green leafy vegetables like spinach or cabbage, that a large panful reduces to a much smaller quantity? The stomach would not be able to cope with such large bulky amounts of raw food. Cooking food **reduces bulk**.

Things to do

5.1 Why do we cook food?

Work in small groups to carry out these investigations.

1 Green leafy vegetables reduce in bulk when cooked.

> You will need:
> portion of cabbage
> scales and masses (weights)
> saucepan and lid
> chopping board
> chopping knife
> measuring jug

What to do
(a) Prepare the cabbage.
 Roll up the leaves tightly and shred very finely with a sharp knife. ⚠
(b) Weigh the shredded cabbage.
 Record the weight.
(c) Record its bulk volume:
 Put the cabbage in the measuring jug. Tap the jug several times. Record the measurement in ml.
(d) Put 4 tablepoons of water in the saucepan. Cover with a lid and bring to the boil.
(e) Add the cabbage. Cover with a lid. Boil for 7 minutes.
(f) Drain off the excess liquid.
 Weigh the cooked cabbage. Record the weight.
(g) Find out the bulk volume of the cooked cabbage. Record findings.
(h) Record your investigation in any appropriate way.
(i) Discuss your results and conclusions with other groups.

2 Investigate the discolouration of food on exposure to the air.

> You will need:
> 1 small potato, scrubbed
> 1 small eating apple
> ½ banana
> pure lemon juice or ½ lemon
> brine (½ level tbsp. salt in 125 ml water)
> white vinegar
> water, cold
> 3 plates, knife, spoon, labels
> 12 dishes/basins or test-tubes

What to do
(a) Place a small cut portion of each food on a plate. Leave exposed to the air.
(b) Place a small cut portion of each food in a container. Cover with cold water. Label and leave.
(c) Repeat the investigation using
 (i) pure lemon juice
 (ii) brine
 (iii) white vinegar.
 Label.
(d) After 15 minutes study each food sample carefully.
(e) Record your investigation in any appropriate way.
(f) Discuss your results and conclusions with other groups.

Further work

1 List the reasons for cooking food.
2 Arrange your list of reasons in an order of priority. Give an explanation for your choice of priority.
3 What do you understand by the term 'perishable foods'?
4 Suggest ways in which the 'life' of these perishable foods can be safely extended:
 (a) milk (b) fruit (c) fish.

Summary

Some foods deteriorate (go bad) quickly. By cooking them we make sure they are safe to eat.

Food

5.2 How is food cooked?

Heat energy is produced when the **molecules** in a substance (liquid, solid or gas) are **excited** (which makes them vibrate or shake more than usual.)
The greater the excitement the more heat is produced.

Heat energy is **transferred** (passed) from a **hotter** to a **cooler** object.
Heat energy is transferred to food when it is cooked by **three methods**.

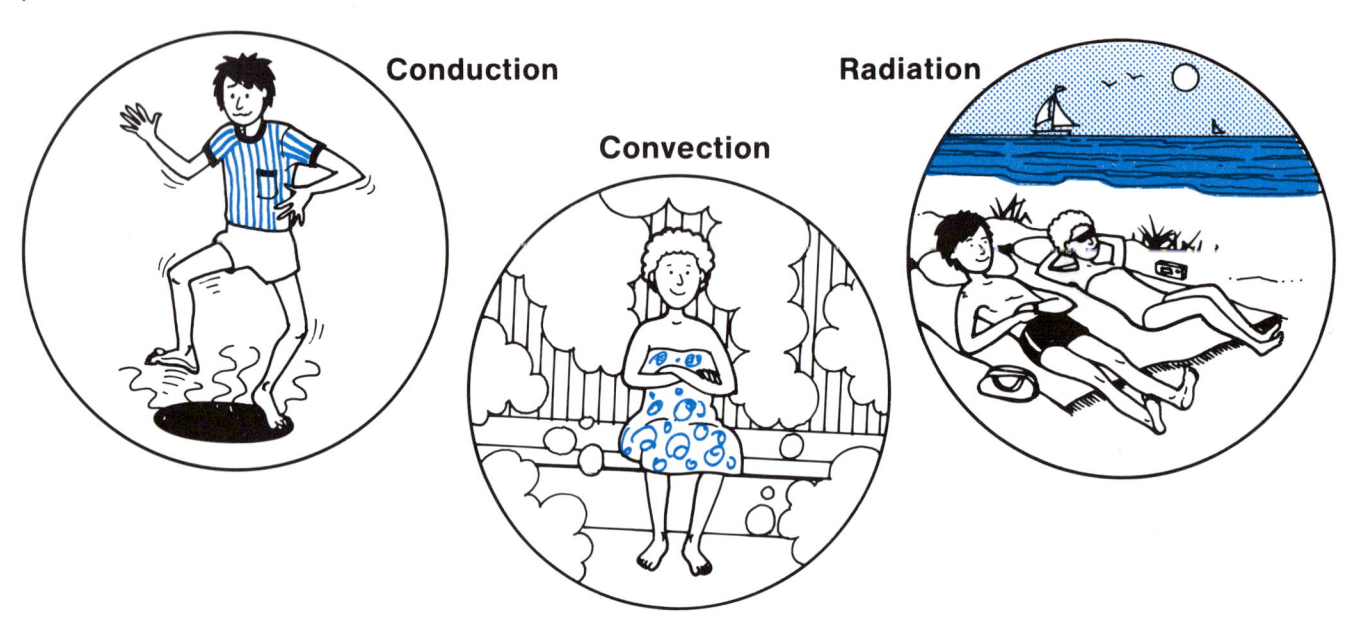

Conduction

Convection

Radiation

Conduction
If you put a rasher of bacon into a frying pan and place it on the gas flame or electric hot plate, the bacon soon starts to sizzle. This is because the base of the pan is heated, causing the **molecules** to **vibrate**. Other molecules close by begin to vibrate also. Gradually the entire pan is heated and this **heat energy** is transferred to the bacon. Heat is **conducted** from molecule to molecule in **solids** and **liquids**.

Convection
Heat energy is passed through **liquids** and **gases** by **convection currents**.
As the molecules in the gas or liquid are heated, they **expand** and **rise**. They are replaced by **cooler, heavier** molecules.

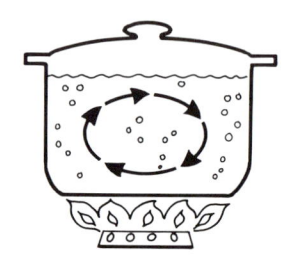

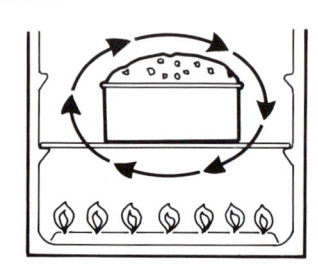

Radiation
Unlike conduction and convection, heat energy transferred by radiation is not passed from molecule to molecule. It passes from one place to another by **rays**. A piece of toast held in front of a fire will turn brown; so will sausages under a grill. They are being cooked by **radiant heat**.

Things to do

5.2 How is food cooked?

Work in small groups to carry out these investigations.

Discover which way heat flows.

1 You will need:
pyrex or plastic bowl
metal spoon
kettle
writing materials

What to do
(a) Boil sufficient water in the kettle to fill the bowl ¾ full. ⚠
(b) Place the metal spoon in the hot water and hold the end of the spoon.
(c) Record your observations and conclusions in any sensible way.

2 You will need:
pyrex or plastic bowl
several ice cubes
metal spoon
writing materials

What to do
(a) Put the ice cubes in the bowl.
(b) Put the metal spoon into the basin and hold the end of the spoon.
(c) Record your observations and conclusions in any sensible way.

3 Devise (work out) an investigation to discover if all substances are good conductors of heat. Use metal, wooden and plastic spoons. Record your observations and conclusions. Discuss your findings with the class.

> Devise (work out) an investigation to discover if all substances are good conductors of heat. Use metal, wooden and plastic spoons.

Further work

We now know that some substances are **good conductors** of **heat energy**.
Other substances are **poor conductors** of heat energy. Poor conductors of heat energy are called **insulators**.

Discover the answers and complete the table below in your book.

Item	Substance it is made from	Good conductor	Poor conductor (insulator)	Why is it a good or poor conductor of heat energy
Duvet or blanket				
Wooden spoon				
Saucepan				
Oven gloves				
Plastic spatula				
Lagging jacket on hot water cylinder				
Still air				

Summary

Heat energy is transferred by (a) conduction (b) convection (c) radiation.

5.3 What makes us want to eat?

We describe anyone who is off their food as having **lost their appetite**. Appetite is essential in making us want to eat. Fortunately most of us have a **healthy appetite**.

Perhaps you can think of a food shop which sets out its goods in an eye-catching and imaginative way.
Some food halls have gained international reputations for their creative skill and expertise. Attractively presented food is big business.
The **appearance** of food plays an important role in persuading us to eat.

◆ Suggest ways in which the colour and texture of food can be used to advantage.

The **smell** of food can arouse **appetite**. Imagine the early morning smell of frying bacon or the warm, comforting smell of freshly baked bread.

There are, of course, smells which have the opposite effect. The smell of sour milk, decaying vegetables, stale meat and fish, and rancid fats warn us that the foods are not fresh and are better avoided.

The **flavour** of food is important.
Flavour is detected by two of our **sense organs**, mainly the **tongue** but also the **nose**.

◆ Have you ever noticed that when you have a head cold, food loses its flavour (taste)?

As we grow older our tolerance of food flavours changes. Food tastes we used to dislike can become ones which we choose and enjoy.

As a result of the **appearance, smell** and **taste** of food, together with a **natural hunger**, our appetite is stimulated. The mouth starts to water as the **saliva** begins to flow in **anticipation** of the food – often quite a time before we actually eat it.

Things to do

5.3 What makes us want to eat?

1 Work in small groups.

Use the following information to devise (work out) a simple investigation to test which areas of the tongue are sensitive to which tastes.

Study the tongue of a member of your group closely.

You will notice that the tongue is covered with **tiny bumps**. Each of these bumps (**a papilla**) bears a sense organ called a **taste bud** at the side.

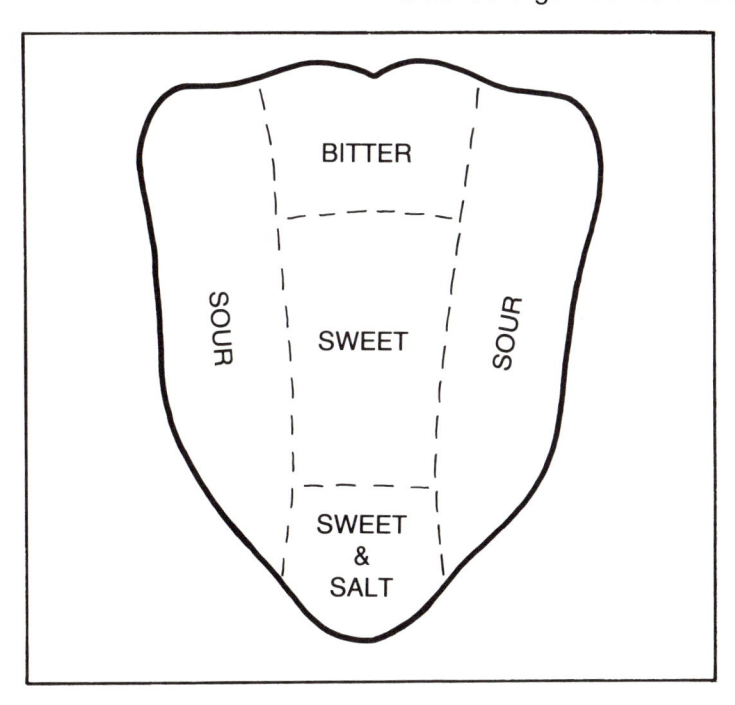

```
        BITTER

SOUR            SOUR
        SWEET


        SWEET
          &
         SALT
```

Look at the diagram.

You will notice that there are **four** different types of taste bud.

What are they?

Taste buds of each type are **grouped** in a **specific area** of the tongue.

Discuss the best way to carry out and record your investigation.

2 Continue to work in small groups.

Devise (work out) a simple experiment to discover what affects our choice of food.

Discuss the best way to carry out and record your investigation.

Give reasons for the choices that people make.

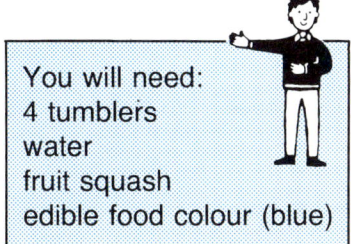

You will need:
4 tumblers
water
fruit squash
edible food colour (blue)

Further work

1 List the food smells which make your mouth water.
2 Describe your favourite food without actually naming it. Think about its colour, appearance, smell, flavour and texture.
3 Sometimes appetite becomes dulled. People who have been ill sometimes have little interest in food.
   What else can dull the appetite?
4 Give examples of the ways in which food retailers persuade us to buy their products by making them attractive to our senses.

Summary

The appearance, smell and taste of food stimulate our appetite.

5.4 What happens to the food we eat?

Most of us eat when we are **hungry** and when our **appetite** is **stimulated** (excited).
Few of us eat for the sole purpose of keeping the body in working order.
Our body cells need the food we eat.
Any food that we do eat has to be **digested** and **broken down** into small particles (molecules) so that it can be **absorbed** into the **blood**. The bloodstream then transports (carries) the absorbed food substances to the parts of the body which need them.

Digestion begins in the **mouth**.
We **bite** and **chew** small pieces of food with our **teeth**.
The food is mixed with **saliva** to moisten it.
After being swallowed, the food is squeezed down the **oesophagus** into the **stomach**.

In the **stomach** the food is mixed with **gastric juice**.
It then passes into the **small intestine**.
It is in the **stomach** and **small intestine** that digestion mainly takes place.
Chemicals in the different **digestive juices** break down the food into small particles.

The **digested** food is **absorbed** (passed) through the walls of the **small intestine** into the **blood**.

Not **all** food is absorbed in this way. Some moves on to the **large intestine**. By this time most of the water and useful food substances have been taken out. The **unused** parts of the food are passed out of the body through the **anus**. This process is called **egestion**.

Egestion takes place about once a day.
By eating plenty of foods containing **dietary fibre**, the water content of the unused substances is increased. This helps to prevent **constipation**.
It also speeds up the passage of unused food through the body.

Things to do

5.4 What happens to the food we eat?

Work on your own.

Prepare an attractive and appetizing snack which has a high dietary fibre content.

> You will need:
> 1 medium-sized potato
> metal skewer
> aluminium foil
> baking tray
>
> *Choice of toppings*
> chopped spring onion and crispy bacon
> coleslaw salad
> baked beans
> cheese, celery and walnut

What to do

1. Set the oven to Gas mark 6, 200°C.
2. Scrub the potato. Dry it well and prick several times with a fork.
3. Push the skewer through the centre of the potato lengthways.
4. Wrap the potato in the aluminium foil. Put on to the baking tray.
5. Put into the oven and bake for about 50 minutes or until the potato is soft. Tidy your work area.
6. When the potato is ready, use oven gloves or an oven cloth to take the baking tray from the oven.
7. Carefully remove the aluminium foil and the skewer. **They will be hot.**
8. Carefully cut the potato across the top.
9. Serve on a plate or napkin with one of the toppings.

Further work

1. Explain why a baked jacket potato is a better food choice than chips.
2. The choice of toppings for the baked potato is varied. How do the toppings add to the dietary fibre content of the snack? 
3. The following diagram shows the jacket potato baking in the oven.

Explain what method of heat transfer takes place in
(a) the skewer
(b) the aluminium foil
(c) the baking tray and oven shelf
(d) the circulation of oven heat.

Summary

To be of use to the body cells food must be digested and then absorbed into the bloodstream.

Family education

6.1 Learning to share: mixing with others

Through **play** the young child **develops skills** which give him/her more **muscle control**, encourage him/her to be **creative** and stimulate his/her **imagination** and **intellect**.

By mixing with other children and adults the child develops his/her **social skills**. The child discovers that he/she is no longer the **centre of attention**. The child learns to **cooperate** and try to **please** others. He/she learns to get along with other children.

Gradually the child becomes **less dependent** upon his/her parents. By about the age of three or four the child is much **less self-centred**. He/she has more **confidence** and is ready to **mix** and **play** with other children.

An important part of learning is that a child comes to recognize the limits of what he/she **may** and **may not do**. This is necessary for the child's own **safety** and for the **comfort** of the **rest of the family**. The child must realize that its behaviour affects other people.

There are several organizations which provide opportunities for **pre-school children** to meet, play and learn together. It is reassuring for parents to know that their child is in the care of **trained adults** or on premises which are **registered**.

Gradually the pre-school child begins to **recognize** and **consider** the feelings of **others**. Through **regular contact** with other children he/she learns to **share** and take his/her turn.

- Pre-school playgroups
- Nursery schools
- Day nurseries
- Nursery classes
- Registered child minders

Find out more about each of these organizations.

Things to do

6.1 Learning to share: mixing with others

Activity 1

Plan some games for a children's party for three to five year olds.
Work in groups.

1. Each group should think of two games and make preparations for them to be played. Your teacher will check that each group is preparing different games.
2. As a class, play the games which each group has planned.
3. Keep a record of each game and assess (judge) its value.
4. To get you started, here are some things to ask about each game.
   Was the game fun?
   Were all the children drawn into the game?
   If someone did not join in, why didn't they?
   Did the game need any special skills?
   Now think of other things to ask.
5. Record your observations and comments in any appropriate way in your exercise book.

Further work

1. Which organizations provide opportunities for pre-school children to meet and play?
2. Suggest other ways in which small children sometimes mix.
3. Suggest ways in which playing games helps a child's development.

Activity 2

Young children are naturally curious. Stimulate (encourage) their curiosity and imagination by starting a Discovery Corner. Build up a collection of small interesting items which will help young children to learn about shape, colour, texture and number.

This is also a good time for children to learn about caring for living creatures. What forms of wildlife would be suitable for them to look after in a classroom?

Summary

Children begin to learn independence and cooperation by mixing with others.

Family education

6.2 Gaining confidence: coping with fears

Throughout the pre-school period a child increases his/her **confidence** and **knowledge** through **play**. Because the experience of play is pleasant, the child finds that **learning** is **enjoyable**.

The more **control** the child has over his/her body, the more his/her **confidence** increases.

Young children are often **boastful** about their achievements. They love **showing off**. They try out and display their new skills of **climbing, balancing** and **swinging**.

They have better control over their hands and fingers. Painting, using scissors and playing with modelling dough improves their skill.

Sometimes their confidence can turn to **aggression** and **bullying**.

However confident they seem, they still feel **insecure** at times. If anything goes wrong or something unexpected happens they will look for **comfort** and **reassurance** from an adult.

At about the age of three or four the child may begin to be afraid of the dark. A bad dream or nightmare might waken him/her. The child's **fear** is increased by the darkness of the room. Suddenly he/she is unhappy about going to bed.

Often all that is needed is **gentle reassurance** and the **security** which comes from having a small light in the room or on the landing.

Never **frighten** or **threaten** a child. A child who feels insecure sometimes regresses (goes back) in his/her development.

Occasionally children of pre-school age do not have a very clear idea of what is theirs and what belongs to others. If they see something they like they expect to be able to have it.

Children must be taught **patiently** and **gently** that they can have only the things which **belong** to them. A child who is punished too severely may learn only to avoid telling the **truth**.

By allowing young children to make small **choices** and **decisions** their **confidence** is increased. They should be allowed to choose what to wear and to dress themselves. They might like to choose somewhere to go for an outing. Encourage them to choose their own bed-time story.

Throughout all this development the child's **personality** has been developing too. What he/she **experiences** in these early years may **influence** the way in which his/her personality develops.

Things to do

6.2 Gaining confidence: coping with fears

Activity 1

Look carefully at these photographs of small children.

Write a few sentences about the personality of the child in each photograph.

Activity 2

Work in groups.

Imagine that your class is a pre-school playgroup or nursery class.

Write short plays which will help young children explore their feelings about: fear of the dark; lying and stealing; bullying other children; being bullied; temper tantrums; sharing toys.

Each group will act their play for the rest of the class.

Further work

1 Spend some time with a young child that you know.
   Watch the child while it is playing.
   Complete the table below to show how the child develops different skills.

Body control skills	Intellectual skills	Creative and imaginative skills	Social skills
Example Cutting out with scissors			

2 What do you think a young child should be capable of doing by the time he/she goes to a nursery school?

Summary

By making small choices and decisions children increase their confidence and independence.

Family education

6.3 Growing up safely: playing

Statistics show that many young children **die** or are **injured** each year as a result of **accidents** which happen in or near the **home**.
In Book 1 we looked at ways in which the home could be made a safer place.

However, many accidents happen **outside** the home. Children are **injured** or **killed** as a result of **falls, road accidents, drowning** and **suffocation** while playing.

Children love to be **adventurous**. They enjoy **climbing, swinging, balancing** and **exploring**. Without having their adventurous spirit crushed they have to understand that there are **dangers**.
Never **underestimate** the dangers of **rivers, streams** and **ponds**. The toddlers' pool at the swimming baths is very different from **fast-flowing** streams and **slimy, steep-sided** ponds.

◆ **Frozen** ponds and streams are extremely dangerous and should never be played on. Why?

Teach children to **swim** from an early age. They must learn not to be afraid of water but must understand its dangers.
Learning about **road safety** is an **essential** part of every child's training.
There have been tragic accidents where young children have been run over by a car or delivery van which was **reversing**.
Some lorries have **automatic** warning bleepers which work when the vehicle is in reverse gear.

◆ Drivers of cars and lorries should always check around their vehicle before moving off. Why?

Most plastic and polythene bags carry warnings about the danger of **suffocation**. They should be kept well out of the reach of young children.

SAFETY FIRST
TO AVOID DANGER OF SUFFOCATION, PLEASE KEEP THIS WRAPPER AWAY FROM BABIES AND CHILDREN.

Children enjoy exploring **enclosed spaces**. Particularly dangerous are old **refrigerators** and **freezers** which have been left in dumps or on waste ground. Some have self-locking doors and it is easy for a young child to become **trapped** and **suffocate**.

Discourage young children from **tunnelling** into **sand, loose earth** and **snow**. Unstable materials like these may easily **collapse**.

Things to do

6.3 Growing up safely: playing

Activity 1

Work as a class.

With your teacher, spend a short time looking around your locality. Note down anything you notice which could be a danger to a pre-school child.

A

Back in the classroom divide into small groups. Each group should concentrate on one of the dangers which you noted.

Write a 'newspaper story' of an imaginary incident linked to the danger you noticed. Illustrate your newspaper article.

Discuss and display the work of all the groups.

Further work

1 Study the potential (possible) danger in each of the situations below.

B

Complete the table.

Danger	Type of injury	Injury caused by
Example Used vehicle dump	Serious cuts	Sharp, rusty metal

2 Suggest how each of the dangers in **B** could be avoided.

3 Many young children travel by car with their family. Suggest ways in which young children can travel as safely as possible.

Summary

Very young children need supervision while they play.

6.4 Growing up safely: people

Sadly we have to accept that there are a small number of people in the community who are prepared to do harm to others. Often their victims are the **young** and **helpless**.

The fact that some of our **streets, parks** and **countryside** are no longer safe places is a constant source of worry to the parents of young children.

A natural part of a child's **development** is to become **independent** and to have **confidence** with adults.

Parents must also teach their children that **some** adults may do them **harm**.

Never **deliberately frighten** children or **threaten** them with situations that might frighten them.

Teach a child that a policeman or policewoman is a **friend**.

Arrange for young children to be **taken to** and **collected from** school or to go in **groups**. Make sure they understand that they **must not** talk to **strangers**. They must **never** accept **sweets** or a **lift** from a **stranger**.

Teach a child that if he/she is approached by a stranger he/she must make as much **noise** as possible and **kick** and **scream**.

There are some areas in this country which operate a **safe-house** scheme.

A safe-house is somewhere children can go if they feel threatened. Safe-houses display a **sticker** in the window.

◆ Occupants of safe-houses and their regular visitors or lodgers are **carefully checked** before they are allowed to display the sticker. Why?

Children may not only be at risk from **strangers**. Sometimes members of their **own family** abuse (ill-treat) them.

There have been several cases where children have been so badly **neglected** and **ill-treated** that they have died.

Some children suffer **sexual abuse** from members of their own family or from people who live in or visit the home.

Occasionally small children can be very trying. There are times when they need to be **punished** for behaving badly or doing wrong.

Try to explain **calmly** to young children what they have done wrong. If possible show them how to put things **right**.

◆ Try to avoid hitting young children. Why?

Things to do

6.4 Growing up safely: people

Activity 1

If possible your teacher will have made arrangements for someone to talk to you about child abuse.

◆ Listen carefully to what he/she has to say and be ready to ask questions.

Activity 2

As a class, discuss the problem of keeping young children safe from people who intend doing them harm.

◆ Use the blackboard to brainstorm ideas to help you.

◆ Try to think of circumstances in which young children might be persuaded to go with strangers.

◆ Try to think of ways in which young children can be made aware of the dangers without frightening them.

Either
Design a poster which reminds young children of the dangers.

or
Write a story to be read to a young child so that he/she understands the dangers and learns how to react to them.

or
Make up and act a short play which will show young children how strangers might approach them and how they should respond. Use puppets to represent the characters in the play. Why?

Further work

1. What signs might arouse your suspicion that a child who lives near you is being ill-treated?
2. Whom could you contact if you thought that a child was being ill-treated or abused in some way?
3. What are the dangers of hitting a young child as a means of correction?

Summary

Teach young children to say 'No' to strangers.

Using tools and equipment

7.1 The cooker: hobs

◆ How frequently is some part of the cooker used in your home? Once or twice a day? For every meal?

The **cooker** is likely to be the piece of kitchen equipment which is used most regularly.

◆ Cookers can be heated by **gas, electricity, oil** and **solid fuel**, although most people choose to use either gas or electricity. Why?

In Book 3 you will learn about **microwave** cookers which are becoming very popular.

The cooker is usually made up of **three** parts or units.

In a **free-standing** cooker all three units are contained in **one** piece of equipment.

Similar units may be bought **separately** and **built into** a range of kitchen fittings. This arrangement of the units is called **split-level**.

◆ Think about the advantages and disadvantages of both styles of cooker.

The **hob** of the cooker is the unit which gets most frequent use.

◆ Look around your local shops and showrooms to see the range of gas and electric hobs that are available.

Electric radiant hobs

The hotplates of radiant hobs have either **coiled radiant rings** or **sealed discs**.

Coiled rings are placed above special reflecting bowls.
The heating element is encased in a metal tube which glows red when hot. ⚠

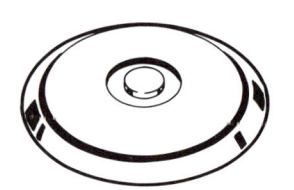

Sealed disc   Radiant ring

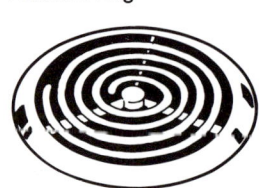

◆ The size of the hotplates may vary. Why?

Sealed disc hobs have a spiral heating element which is covered by a solid metal plate and sealed to the hob.
Some sealed discs have a central **sensor** which keeps the temperature of the plate even, for gentle cooking.

Ceramic hobs are made from a smooth, flat sheet of **toughened glass**. The **heating areas** are marked on the surface and are usually of different sizes. Coiled **heating elements** are placed **under** the glass.
Hotplates on ceramic hobs take a little longer to heat up and cool down.

Ceramic hob

Gas hobs

Gas hobs usually have four **burners** of differing sizes to suit different pans.
Gas burners are **easily controlled** and give **instant heat** which can be **clearly seen**.
Modern gas cookers have **electric spark ignition** either from a battery or from the mains electricity supply.
For **easy cleaning** gas cookers are fitted with removable spillage trays which are fitted under each burner.

Things to do

7.1 The cooker: hobs

Activity 1

Work in small groups to investigate gas and electric hobs.

Study the hobs you have been allocated and complete the table below.

Type of cooker fuel used	Type of hob	Number and size of hotplates or burners	Hob controls; type and ease of use	Heat control	Ease of cleaning	Comments on safety

1. Find out how the fuel reaches the cookers you have been looking at.
2. Make a diagram of the hob control panel on the cookers you have been investigating. How do they differ? If they incorporate any safety features say what they are.
3. Are any economy features incorporated into the hobs you have been looking at?
4. Make a list of differences you noticed when an electric hotplate and a gas burner were in use.

Activity 2

Carry out this timing investigation.

> You will need:
> 1 small saucepan
> 250 ml cold water
> clock or watch
> paper and pencil

What to do

1. Measure the water into the saucepan.
2. Place the pan on a **suitable** electric hotplate. Switch on to the hottest setting.
3. Time how long it takes for the water to reach boiling point.
4. Empty the pan. ⚠
5. Make sure the pan is **cold**. Why? Repeat the investigation using a gas burner.
6. Record this investigation in your book.

Further work

Refer to the timing investigation you carried out.
1. How did you know when the water had reached boiling point? Describe what you saw.
2. How long did it take for the water to reach boiling point on the electric hotplate?
3. How long did it take for the water to reach boiling point on the gas burner?
4. Give reasons for any differences?

5. What methods of heat transference took place?
6. Design a pan which you could use on both a gas and an electric hob.
    (a) In red label any safety features that you think should be included.
    (b) In blue label any features which are linked to economy.

Summary

Learn to use hobs safely and economically.

Using tools and equipment

7.2 The cooker: the grill

Grilling is a method of cooking food by **radiant** heat.

Grills on **electric** cookers are usually placed

(a) below the hob   (b) at eye level

(c) above or below the built-in oven.

The **heating element** in the grill usually heats the whole of the grill pan area so that **large quantities** of food can be grilled at a time.

For **convenience** and **economy** some grills have a **dual circuit** control so that only part of the grill need be heated for small amounts of food.

Some modern electric grills can be used as a second, smaller oven. When the heating element is not being used to grill food the grill space can be heated by additional elements.

◆ What is the advantage of this?

◆ Look carefully at an electric grill. Find out how to heat it.
How long does it take to heat up fully?
Can the grill space be used as a second oven?
Is there a dual heating circuit?
Is the grill pan well balanced? Can it be handled safely and easily?

◆ Find pictures of other pieces of equipment which are used to grill food.

On **gas** cookers the grill is usually situated

(a) at eye level (some of them have a fold-away feature)   (b) at waist level.

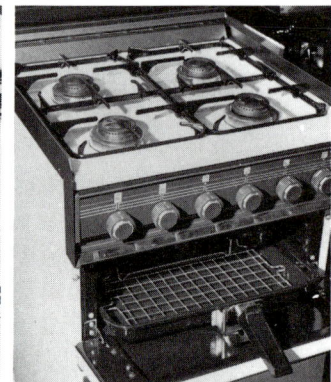

Gas grills are heated either by **grill frets** or by a **gauze plate**.

◆ Look carefully at your gas cooker and decide which of these features it uses.

◆ Find out how to operate the grill.
How long does it take to heat up fully?
Does it have any special economy features?
Study the design of the grill pan. Are there any special safety features?

◆ Find out if there are any attachments for gas and electric grills which will extend their usefulness.

Things to do

7.2 The cooker: the grill

Activity 1

Practise using the grill.
Make a toasted cheese snack.

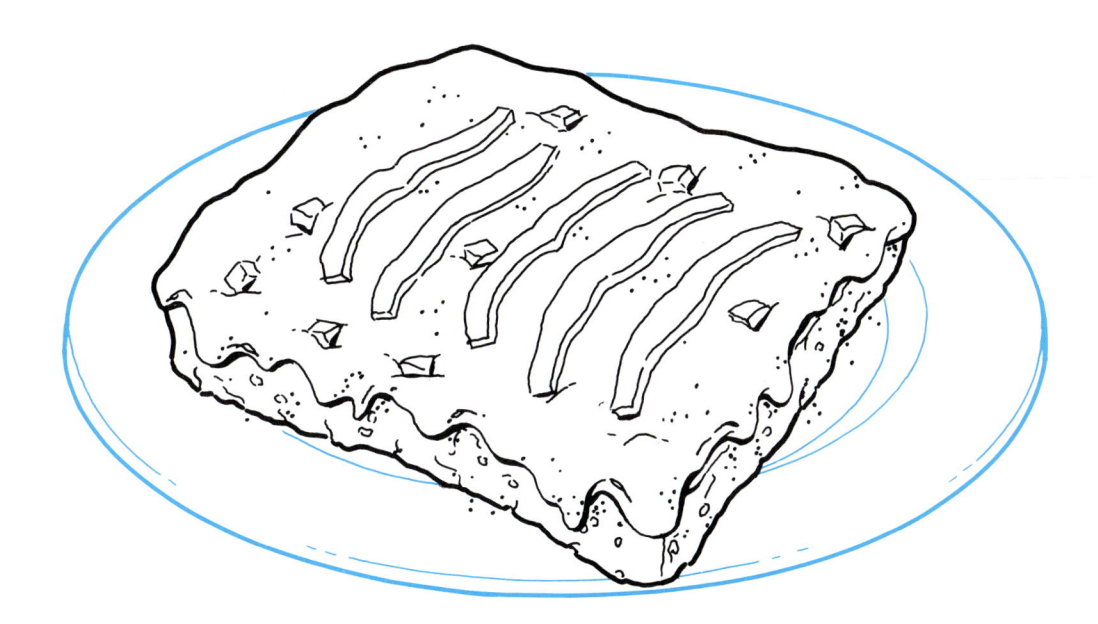

You will need (per person):
1 thick slice wholemeal bread
Topping
25 g Edam cheese, grated
1 sm. tomato, deseeded and chopped
2–3 thin slices onion, chopped
pinch mixed herbs
Garnish
thin slices of red and green pepper

What to do

1. Here is a list of instructions which you must follow. They are not written in their correct order.
2. Study the list and write out in your exercise book the **correct** order for doing the job.
3. Follow your instructions to complete the task.
   (a) Spread the topping mixture on the untoasted side of the bread.
   (b) Set a place at the table.
   (c) Pre-heat the grill.
   (d) Collect the equipment and ingredients.
   (e) Toast the bread on one side only.
   (f) Prepare the topping mixture. Mix together well.
   (g) Put the serving plate in a warm place.
   (h) Switch off the grill.
   (i) Serve on a warm plate garnished with thinly sliced peppers.
   (j) Replace under the grill and cook until golden brown and bubbling.

Further work

1. Suggest reasons why this snack is a good food choice.
2. If you wanted to make a similar snack using an infra-red (contact) grill, how would you adapt the ingredients?
3. Suggest alternative fillings for a toasted sandwich made on an infra-red grill.
4. Use the grill at home to find out what happens to a slice of bread which you
   (a) grill on alternate sides for a few seconds at a time until golden
   (b) grill on one side only until golden and then on the other side
   (c) grill until very dark brown.

Describe the differences that you can see. Try to give reasons for what has happened?

Summary

Understand how equipment works.

Using tools and equipment

7.3 The cooker: the oven

◆ How would you describe an oven?

An oven is simply a **well insulated**, steel box which comes in a variety of attractive, hard-wearing, easily cleaned finishes.

Most ovens have specially coated **linings** which make them **easier to clean** or prevent splashes from burning on.

In both **gas** and **electric** ovens food is cooked by **convection currents** which are produced by the heat source. As warmed air expands and rises it displaces colder air.

Gas ovens

In order to produce **heat** gas has to **burn**. A gas cooker must have a good supply of **air** for the burning fuel.

As there are dangerous **by-products** from the burning process a gas cooker must also have a **flue**.

As a result of the way in which heat is produced in a gas cooker strong **convection currents** are set up. These create **heat zones** within the oven. The area of the oven around the **middle** shelf will be at the **chosen** oven setting. The **top** shelf will be **hotter** and the **lower** part of the oven will be **cooler**.

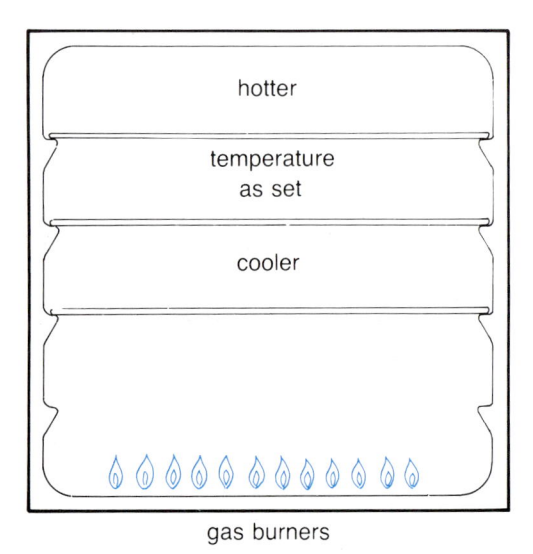

[Diagram: gas oven cross-section showing "hotter" at top shelf, "temperature as set" at middle shelf, "cooler" at lower shelf, with gas burners at bottom]

gas burners

◆ Look carefully at your gas oven. Identify (a) the gas burner, (b) the opening for fresh air to enter, (c) the flue.

◆ Look in recipe books. Select three dishes needing **different** oven settings which could be cooked in a gas oven **at the same time**. Explain your reasons for choosing these dishes.

Electric ovens
Conventional electric ovens have **heating elements** at the sides behind metal panels which come out for easy cleaning.

Because the heating elements **radiate** heat into the oven, the **convection currents** which are set up are not as strong as those in a gas oven. This means that the **heat zones** are less obvious.

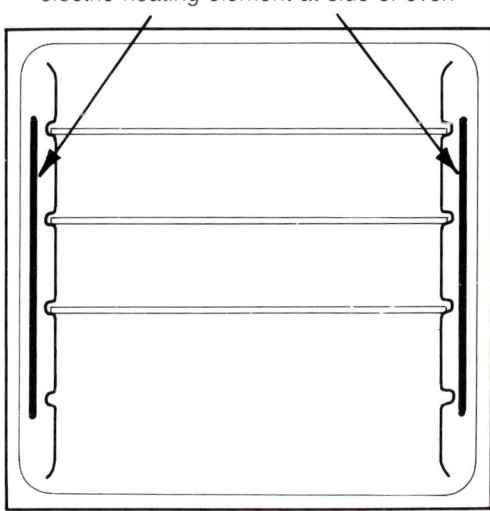

[Diagram: conventional electric oven showing electric heating element at side of oven]

electric heating element at side of oven

Fan-assisted electric ovens **cook the food more quickly, distribute the heat more evenly** and can be run at **lower temperatures**, so are more **economical**.

In a fan-assisted oven there is a **circular heating element** at the **back** of the oven placed around a **fan**. The fan circulates the heated air and ensures that there is an **even temperature** throughout the oven.

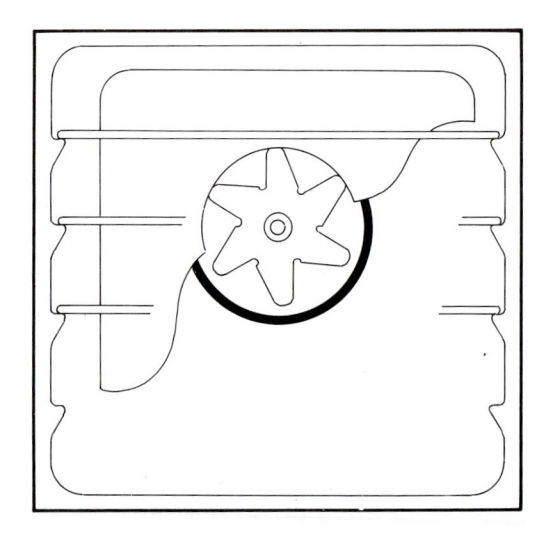

[Diagram: fan-assisted oven showing circular heating element around fan at back]

◆ When could this be an advantage?

◆ Look carefully at both types of electric oven.

Things to do

7.3 The cooker: the oven

Activity 1

Work in small groups.

Investigate heat zones in a gas cooker.
Make a batch of scones from a standard recipe or from a recipe which your teacher will give you.
Decide how you will carry out your investigation.

Answer the following questions.
1. Was there any variation in cooking time? If so, give details.
2. Is there any variation in the colour of the finished scones? If so, give reasons why.
3. You will notice that the scones have risen. Work out the average height of the scones at each shelf position used.
4. Does the texture of the finished scones vary in any way?

Discuss your investigation with the other groups.

Activity 2

Work in small groups.

Investigate conventional and fan-assisted electric ovens.
Make a batch of small cakes (by the creaming method) from a standard recipe or from a recipe which your teacher will give you.
Cook part of the batch in the upper and lower areas of both types of electric oven.
Decide how you will carry out and record your investigation.

Answer these questions.
1. What is the required oven temperature setting for the cakes in each type of oven?
2. How long did each oven take to reach its required temperature?
3. How long did the cakes take to cook in (a) the conventional oven, (b) the fan-assisted oven?
4. Describe the physical properties of each batch of cooked cakes. Try to account for any differences.

Discuss your results and conclusions with the other groups.

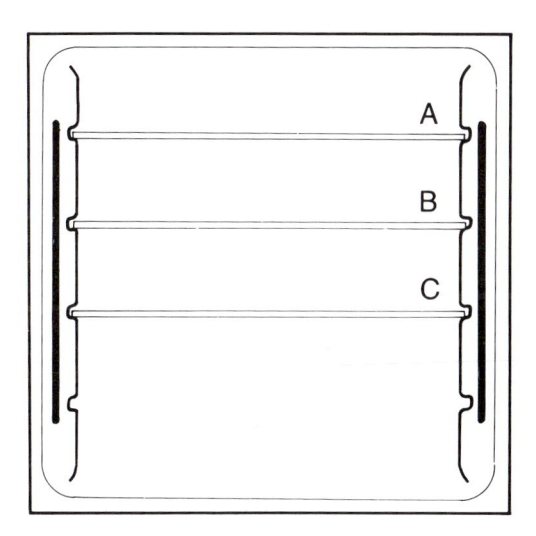

Further work

1. Now that you have thought about and practised using the cooker, you are better able to make informed choices.
   (a) Visit your local shops and showrooms and look at the cookers that are available.
   (b) Ask for brochures which describe the features of the various cookers. Study them.
   (c) In your book draw the model of cooker which you think would best suit the needs of your family.
2. Complete the table below.

Model of cooker chosen	Fuel used	Features of chosen model	Reasons for choice
Example	Electricity	Waist-level grill	All members of family small in height

3. Use a library or contact your local multicultural centre to find out about cooking facilities in other countries.

Summary

A cooker is the most frequently used piece of kitchen equipment. Choose wisely.

Using tools and equipment

7.4 Using the sewing machine

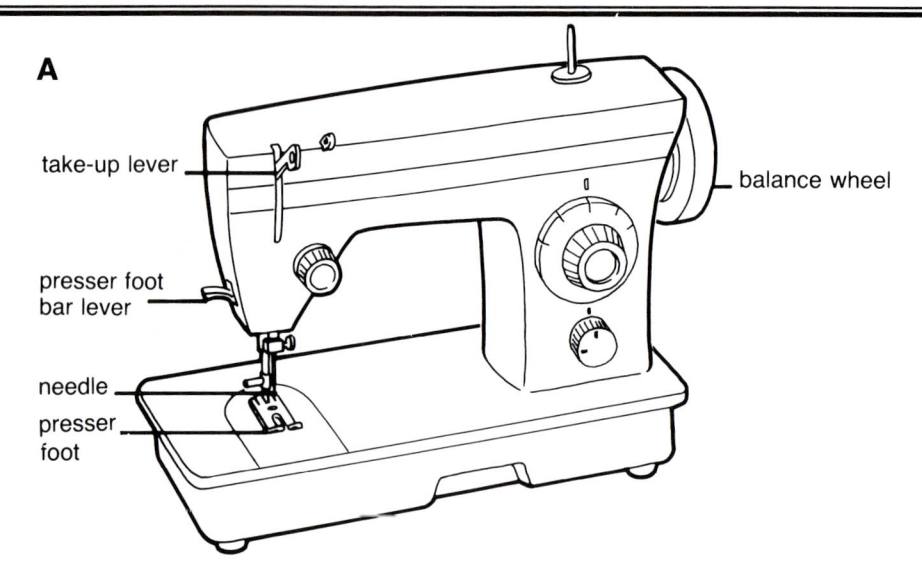

A

- take-up lever
- balance wheel
- presser foot bar lever
- needle
- presser foot

When you use a sewing machine in school it may well look like the one in diagram **A**.

This machine is called a **swing needle sewing machine** because as well as being able to produce a **straight** stitch called a **lock stitch** the needle can also swing from side to side to produce a **zig-zag stitch**.

In order to get the best use from your sewing machine you need to know what it can do and to **practise** controlling it.

Look carefully at your machine to see how it is operated.

To get some idea of what the machine can do, carry out this investigation.

Investigation

Work in small groups.

⚠ **Only one person** should operate the sewing machine at a time.

1. If you have a choice of presser foot, select the one which is designed for straight stitching (lock stitch) and attach it to the sewing machine.

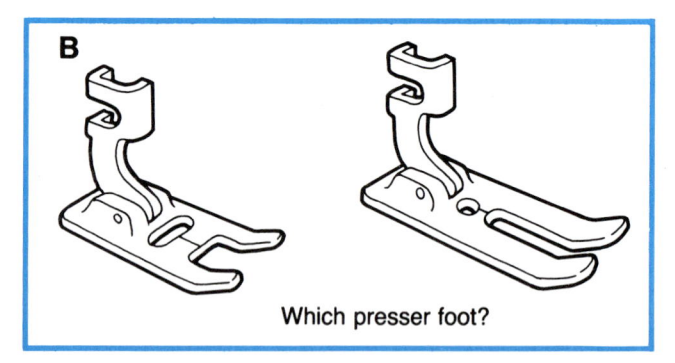

B

Which presser foot?

2. Do not use any thread in the machine.
3. Use a piece of material which will show clearly the perforations made by the sewing machine needle.

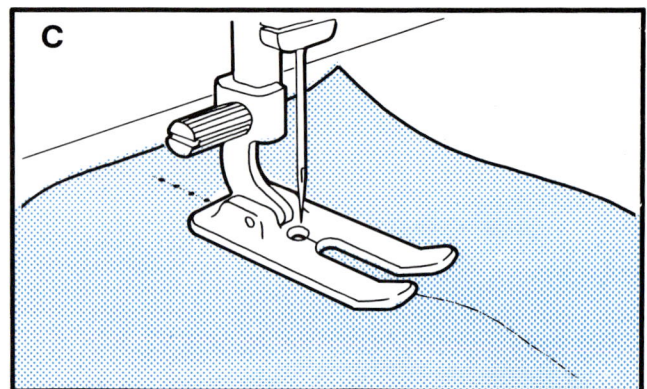

C

4. When you are ready to sew, the machine and material will be in the position shown in diagram **C**.
   (a) Find out how fast you can make the machine operate safely.
   (b) Imagine you are in a slow bicycle race and see how slowly you can make the machine go forward.
   (c) Decide on a number below ten and sew only that number of stitches. Do this several times.
   (d) Practise sewing along straight lines. Try going round a few curves. Find out the best way to turn a right-angled corner.
   (e) Can you make the machine stop with the needle in the work?
   (f) Find out what happens when you press the reverse button or lever.
   (g) What function have your hands been performing all this time?

   Continue to practise these skills until you are satisfied that you can control the machine.

5. Now you are ready to try with the machine **threaded**.
6. Practise using a straight stitch (lock stitch) on fabrics of **different** constructions.

Things to do

7.4 Using the sewing machine

Activity 1

Design need Tools tend to become scattered. When preparing to carry out a task it is frustrating to have to search for the tools needed.

Design brief Design and make a simple wallet to hold a set of tools for carrying out a specific task. Make this wallet using the materials you have been given.

> These materials are available:
> piece of strong, closely woven cotton fabric, 700 mm × 350 mm
> reel of tacking cotton
> reel of sewing cotton
> scissors, pins, sewing needle
> sewing machine
> machine needle, size 90/14

What to do

1. Book 1, Unit 9.4 will remind you about the detailed thinking and planning which you must do to carry out a design brief.
2. Spend some time thinking about how to solve the design need.
   Here are some questions to ask yourself to get started.

◆ What type of tools will be kept in the wallet? Make a list.

◆ Are the tools all the same size?

◆ What is the most sensible way of storing these tools in the wallet: jumbled up, separately, in twos?

◆ How can you prevent the tools from falling out of the wallet?

◆ Consider appearance, cost and size.

3. In your book make a series of drawings and statements to show your plan of action.
4. Write out your plan of action on one side of a sheet of plain A4 paper using the headings in this diagram.

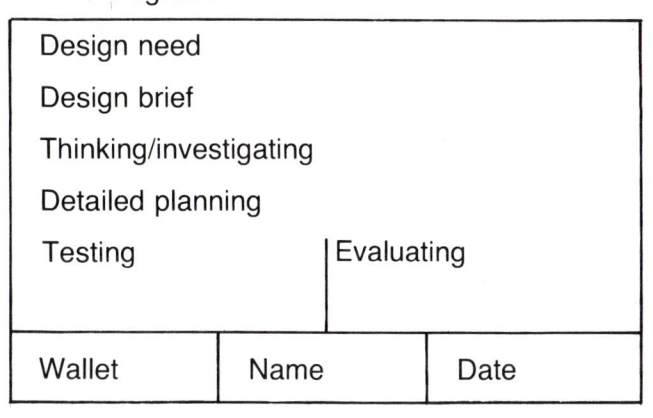

Design need		
Design brief		
Thinking/investigating		
Detailed planning		
Testing	Evaluating	
Wallet	Name	Date

Further work

1. Look carefully at the fabric samples on which you practised using the sewing machine.
   Is a straight stitch (lock stitch) suitable for all types of fabric. Give reasons for your answers.
2. Look again at each presser foot in diagram **B**. Explain the difference in design.
3. Why were you given a size 90/14 sewing machine needle?
4. Suggest ways other than stitching in which textiles may be joined. Give examples.
5. Design some sewing machine practice charts which will extend your skills in machine control.

Summary

Learn the capabilities of your sewing machine and practise your machining skills.

8.1 Designing for safety

Many accidents happen in the home.
As **designers** we have an important part to play in designing **for safety**. When solving a design brief always design with **safety** in mind. Make notes about safety as part of your work in solving the design problem.

How can poor design result in dangerous products?

◆ Keep an eye open for any newspaper articles which report accidents caused by poor design.

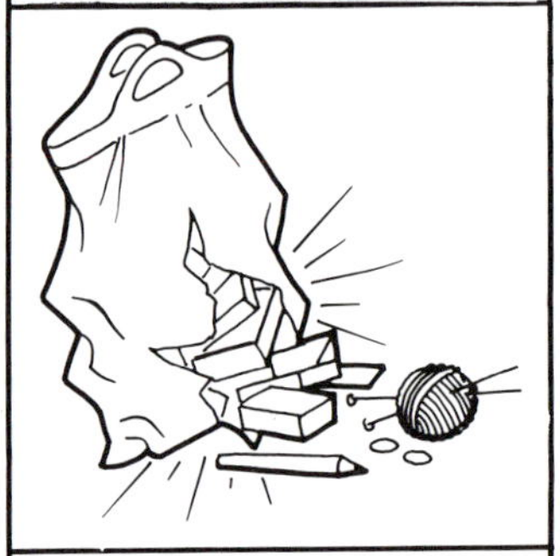

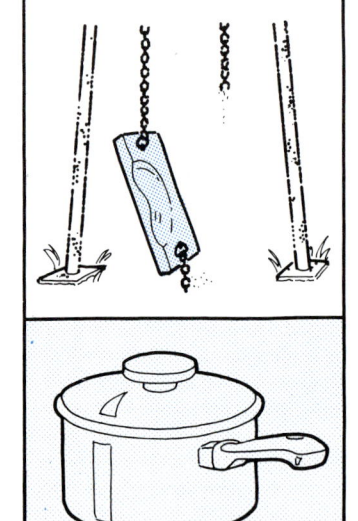

Sharp edges and corners may cause cuts and bruises. Even if the design is one which will not be handled, all sharp edges and corners should be **rounded off**. As well as being safer the design will be more **aesthetically pleasing**.

Materials vary in **strength** and are suitable for different purposes. Choose sensibly. Sometimes it helps to make a model or to experiment to find out about strength problems.

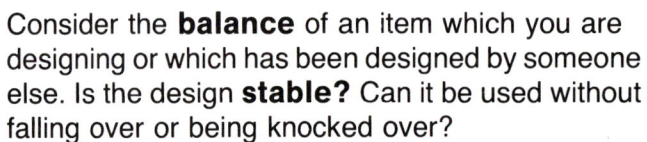

Consider the **balance** of an item which you are designing or which has been designed by someone else. Is the design **stable?** Can it be used without falling over or being knocked over?

Sometimes the safety of an item may be affected by **corrosion** or **decay**. As a result of repeated use parts of the design may be weakened by movement and flexing. Well designed items will be made from **suitable materials**. Their **moving parts** which may become worn will be **replaceable**.

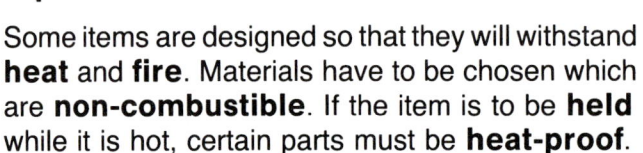

Some items are designed so that they will withstand **heat** and **fire**. Materials have to be chosen which are **non-combustible**. If the item is to be **held** while it is hot, certain parts must be **heat-proof**.

Electricity is very useful but when it is used **carelessly** or with **faulty equipment** it becomes a **killer**. If you are designing items which are operated by electricity, check that **water** cannot get into any part of the circuit.

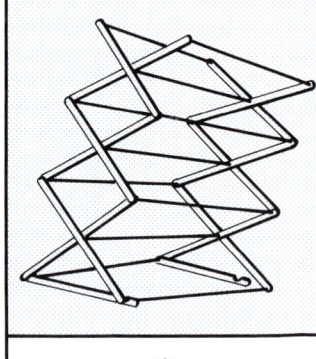

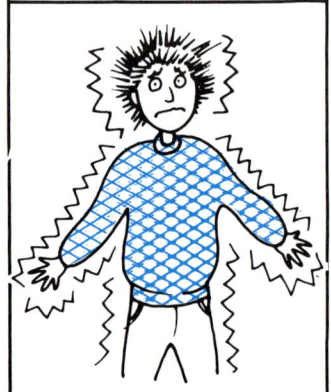

Sometimes **poor instructions** can cause unnecessary danger. When directions or instructions for use come with an item they must be **clear, accurate, simple** and **easily understood**.

Things to do

8.1 Designing for safety

Activity 1

1. Re-read the previous page.
2. Identify the features which should be considered when analysing (studying in detail) the design of an item.
3. Write down these features to make a checklist.

Activity 2

1. Choose some household items and, using the checklist which you have made, analyse (study) the design of the items. Handle each of the items if this is possible.

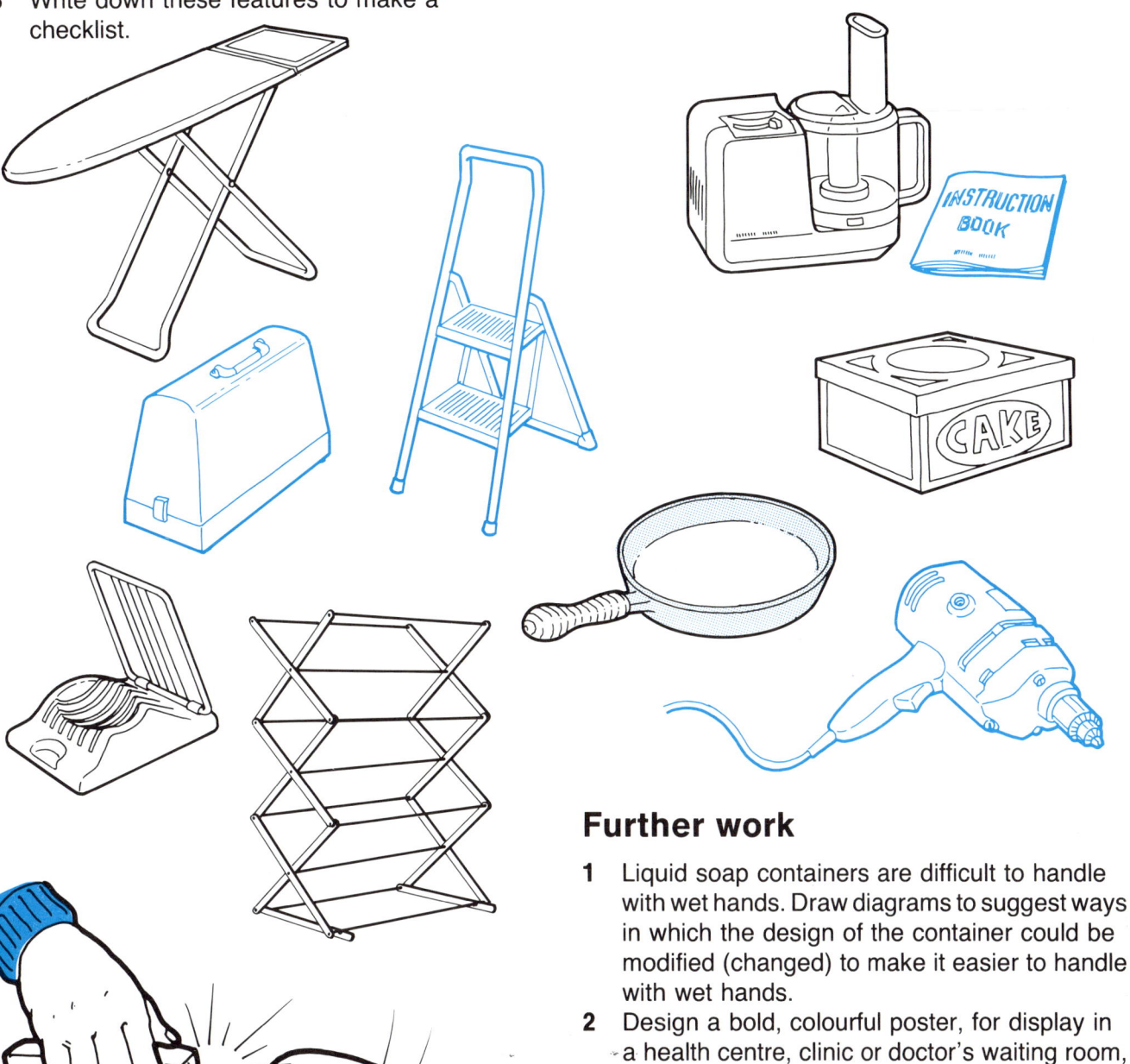

Further work

1. Liquid soap containers are difficult to handle with wet hands. Draw diagrams to suggest ways in which the design of the container could be modified (changed) to make it easier to handle with wet hands.
2. Design a bold, colourful poster, for display in a health centre, clinic or doctor's waiting room, which makes people aware of the need for safety in design.
3. Write an account of a recent accident in your home or that of a relative which happened as a result of the poor design of an item.

Summary

Designing for safety is an important aspect of a designer's task.

Design for living

8.2 Designing for the handicapped

Human beings are capable of a **wide range** of **complex** (difficult) **movements**. They can crawl, walk, run, lie down, sit, sprawl and kneel. They can reach forwards, sideways and upwards, can grip and grasp and perform a range of complicated actions with hand-held tools.
In order to function (work) **efficiently** they need a certain level of **comfort** and **warmth**.

Because human beings walk upright on two legs, **balance** is important.

Height, weight, sitting and lying positions, size, reach and hand movements present designers with a wide range of design needs.

Some or all of the **senses** of hearing, vision, smell, taste and touch must be satisfied by design.

In **old** or **handicapped** people, one or more of these senses might be impaired (damaged) or not functioning. In such cases the need for **comfort** and **warmth** is even more relevant.

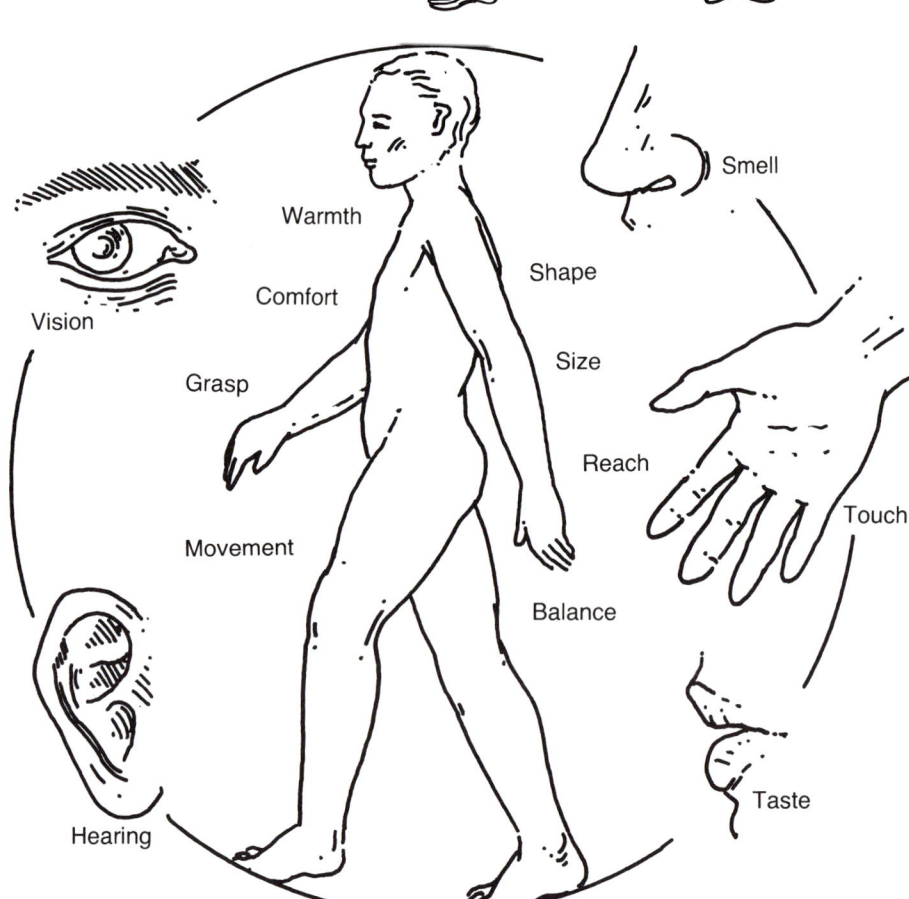

The first stage of any design calls for careful study of body size and movements. This is called **anthropometrics**.

The purpose of all design is to make life better in some way. Close **consultation** with the person or persons for whom the item is being designed is necessary to make sure that a satisfactory result is achieved.

Things to do

8.2 Designing for the handicapped

Activity 1

Blind people often rely on touch in order to 'see'.

◆ Design and make a simple game for use by a blind person.

Activity 2

A person in a wheelchair may wish to do some cooking. A recipe book is often difficult to read when laid flat.

◆ Design a holder for a recipe book which will overcome this problem.

Activity 3

Young or old may be handicapped by arthritis. Wrist and finger movements are difficult and painful. The simple job of peeling potatoes or opening a screw-top jar becomes a major task.

◆ Design a device to help those suffering from arthritis to peel potatoes or open a screw-top jar.

Activity 4

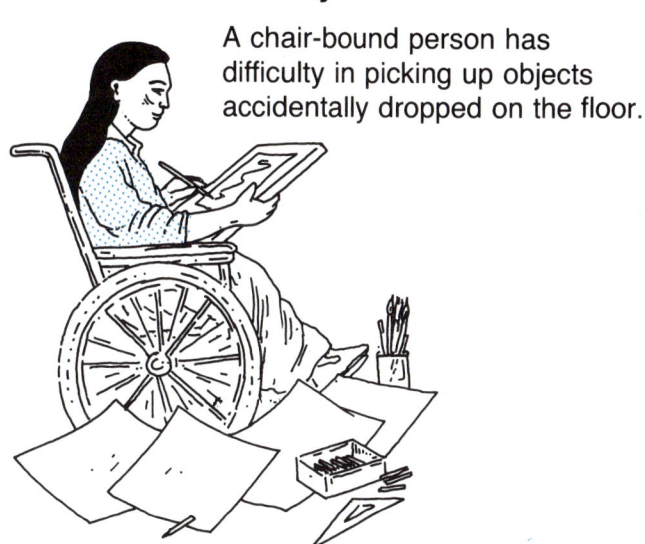

A chair-bound person has difficulty in picking up objects accidentally dropped on the floor.

◆ Design a device to help him/her pick up objects dropped on the floor.

Further work

1. Why is it necessary to give special consideration to designing for handicapped people?
2. Sketch your own hand. Measure span, length, finger size, etc. Compare the shape and size with the hand of another member of your family.
   Record your observations.
   Is there any difference in the range of activities you can each perform with your hands? Make a list.
3. Look at simple objects such as scissors, door handles, kitchen implements and bathroom accessories. Sketch them.
   Discuss how they are held and used.
   Discuss their use by people with a wide range of handicaps.

Summary

Designers aim to improve the user's quality of life.

64 *Design for living*

8.3 Using colour

Wherever we look we can see **colour**. We are surrounded by it. Colour has been so much a part of our lives that many of us take it for granted.

It is worth stopping to think about the ways in which we **use** colour as well as recognizing the ways in which colour can **affect** us. Colour affects our **emotions** and our **moods**. It has been suggested that there are more suicides during long spells of overcast weather conditions.

◆ What colours do you associate with these words:
springtime, death, wedding, depression, seaside, heat-wave, ice?

If colour has such an important effect upon us, we should consider its use carefully when we are designing **colour schemes** for our homes. There are really no **right** or **wrong** colours. The colours we choose express our personality and individuality.
Some combinations of colours may be more suited to particular surroundings but there are no hard and fast rules.

Colour can be used to stimulate (cause) **excitement**. The bull does not see the colour but the crowd is stimulated and excited by the sight of the red cloak.

Colour is used for **identification**.

◆ Think of other examples.

We often use colour to give **information**.

Colour is also used to create **atmosphere**.

Using colour is also big business.

◆ Think of ways in which **advertisers** and **manufacturers** use colour when they want us to buy their products.
You will have noticed that certain colours become very **fashionable** for a time. They are soon replaced by other fashionable colours.

◆ Why does this happen?

◆ What trends have you noticed in car colours recently?

Things to do

8.3 Using colour

Activity 1

You will need:
2 pieces of drawing paper 150 mm × 200 mm
templates of geometric shapes
pencil, rubber
coloured pencils

What to do

1. Use the geometric templates to create a crazy-paving picture on each piece of drawing paper.
2. On paper **A** colour in the shapes with colours which **contrast** sharply.
3. On paper **B** select colours which **tone** to colour in the shapes.
4. Study the different effects of colour in the two pictures.
   Make use of the colour wheel from Unit 8.1.

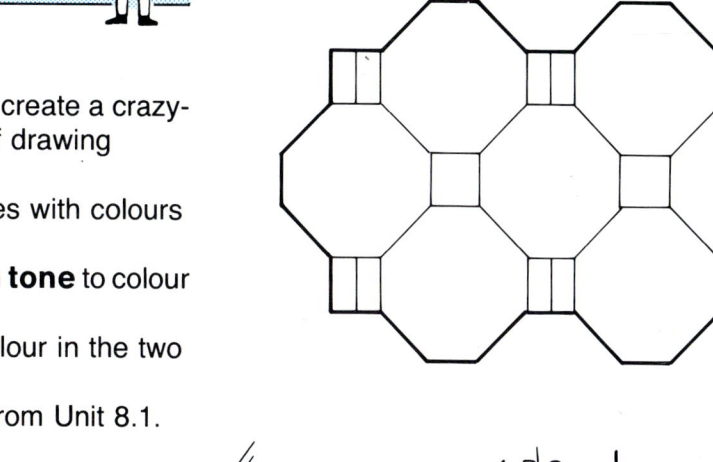

Activity 2

1. Select a colour scheme for this study-bedroom which faces west.
   State the colours you have chosen and give reasons for your choice.
2. If this room faced north, would your choice of colour scheme be altered in any way?
   Give reasons for any changes you would make.

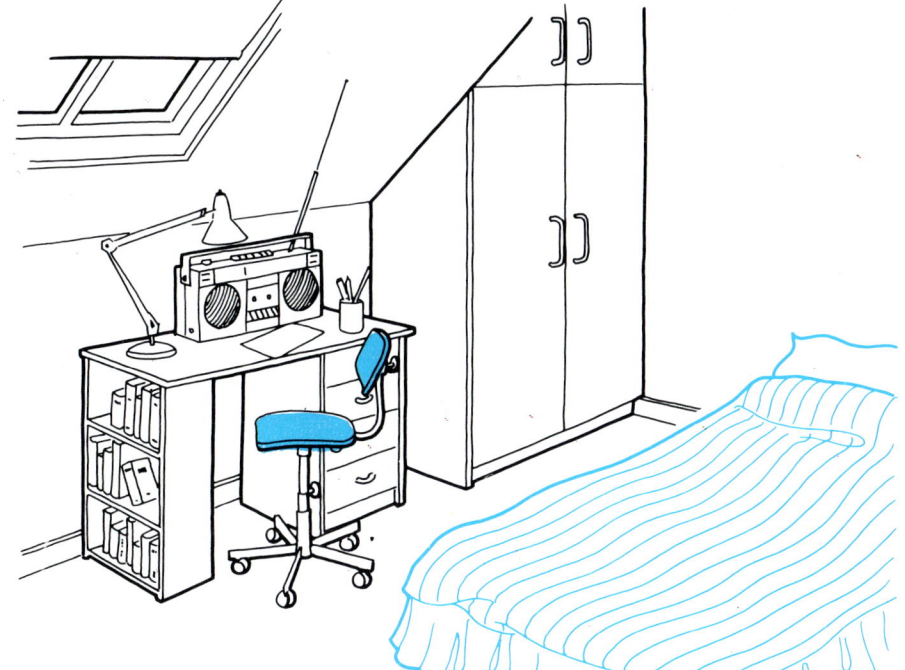

Further work

1. Look in magazines or paint manufacturers' brochures to find examples of rooms using different colour themes.
   Stick some pictures into your book and describe what kind of atmosphere is created in each room setting.
2. Visit your local supermarket. Study the display shelves.
   To which items is your attention drawn? What colour are they?
   Why do you think you noticed them immediately?
3. What factors influence colour choice for the home?

Summary

Our reaction to colour can affect our feelings and moods.

Design for living

8.4 Designing to solve problems

Designs evolve (come about) as the result of a **need**. Remember that early man **designed** simple tools because he **needed** to outwit animals which were stronger and faster (Book 1). The situations below illustrate a problem (need). Design solutions which fulfil the need.

1 You have just bought a one litre bottle of **concentrated** fabric softener (**A**).
You decide to dilute the concentrated fabric softener with water in the ratio 1:3 and to store it, ready for use, in these two bottles. Explain how you will solve this problem using only one additional piece of equipment.

3 Your grandmother loves pot plants. She has filled up all the available places on window-ledges and tables.
Design a variety of plant-holders which will allow your grandmother to have more plants and which will make certain the plants get enough light.

2 Your father often supports his feet on a pile of fishing magazines. Your mother complains about the mess. She also finds the magazines heavy to move. However, she understands your father's need to rest his legs and his wish not to throw away the fishing magazines. Design a suitable solution to this problem.

4 Your sister enjoys knitting. She often loses her knitting needles.
Design a suitable container which will let her find the needles she needs easily.
Explain why you think you have solved your sister's problem.

Things to do

8.4 Designing to solve problems

5 An elderly neighbour has a tiny kitchen with cupboards that are too high to reach without a chair. He knows that this is dangerous but feels that he does not have room for both a chair and a set of steps in his kitchen. Solve his problem.

6 Your parents have bought a polished dining table. Your mother is anxious that hot plates and dishes do not mark its surface.
Design a solution which is attractive, practical and inexpensive.

7 You frequently lose the top of your ball-point pen when it rolls off the desk or table on which you are working.
Solve this design fault by designing a pen which does not have this problem but which is still comfortable to hold.

8 Candles often feature as decorative centre pieces on a table or are placed on shelves, room dividers, sideboards, etc. A well-designed candle holder adds to the attractiveness of the candle.
Design candle holders which will take both a number of candles and just one candle.

Further work

What design need prompted these solutions?

Summary

We design solutions to problems.

Fibres and fabrics

9.1 Understanding colour

Everything around has **colour**.
Have you ever wondered where colour comes from?
Colour comes from the **light** which is all about us.
The **Sun** gives us light.
Sunlight (white light) seems to have no colour of its own. However, it can be **split up** so that all its component colours (the colours in it) can be seen. This is what has happened when a **rainbow** appears in the sky.
Red, orange, yellow, green, blue, indigo and **violet** are present in white light.
There is a mnemonic (catch phrase) to help you remember the colours of the rainbow.
Richard **O**f **Y**ork **G**ave **B**attle **I**n **V**ain.

Objects around us **appear** to have a **particular colour** because of the way they react to **sunlight** (white light).
Some objects will **absorb** one or more colours from the white light and will **reflect** a mixture of the other colours. For example, if an object absorbs **yellow** light, it will reflect a **combination** (mixture) of all the other colours **except** yellow. The **reflected light** is what you **see**.
If an object you are looking at is **blue**, it is because the **blue light** is being **reflected**.

◆ What colours will have been absorbed?

Remember also that colours react differently to **temperature**. **Dark** colours **absorb** heat while **light** colours **reflect** heat.

◆ Do you have a favourite colour?

◆ When you last bought new clothes how important was colour?

Look through a selection of fashion magazines or clothes catalogues. Try to identify **colour trends** for a particular year.

◆ Can you think of reasons why colour trends vary **from year to year?**

◆ Is there any noticeable change in colour trends **from season to season?** Try to give explanations.

◆ Are there fashionable colours in products other than clothes?

Look at the colour wheel.
Red, yellow and blue are called **primary** colours. These colours cannot be made by mixing.
Secondary colours are made by mixing **two** of the **primary** colours together. For example, if you mix red with blue you get purple.
Tertiary colours are **shades** of colour which are a result of mixing **secondary** colours. For example, if you mix orange with purple you will get a warm brown colour.
This is only **one** way of grouping colours.

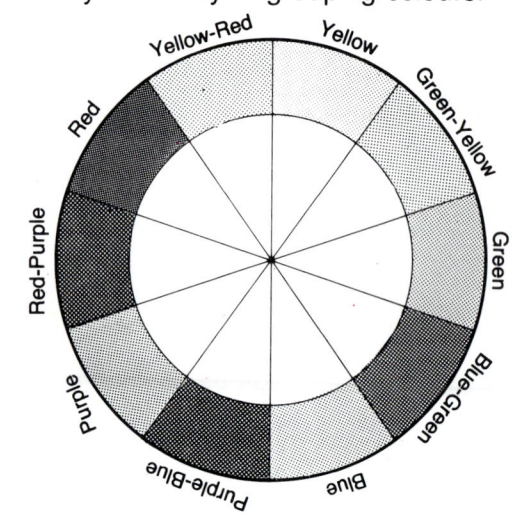

Things to do

9.1 Understanding colour

Activity 1

Investigate colour.

You will need:
coloured paper with adhesive back
paper or card for mounting
pencil, rubber, ruler, scissors

What to do
1. Select a piece of adhesive paper in a **primary** colour.
2. Cut out a square 150 mm × 150 mm.
3. Choose any **secondary** colour. Cut out four 50 mm squares and stick them on to the square of primary colour.
4. Label the primary and secondary colours clearly.
5. Mount and display your work.

Activity 2

Investigate colour.

You will need:
drawing paper
ruler, pencil, rubber
coloured pencils, crayons or paints
paper or card for mounting

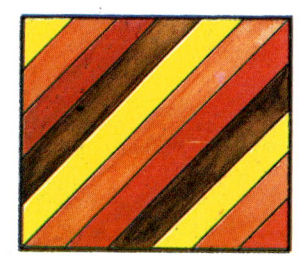

What to do
1. On your drawing paper draw a rectangle 150 mm × 180 mm.
2. Draw in diagonal lines at 20 mm intervals as shown in the diagram.
3. Choose 3 or 4 colours which **harmonize** to colour in the stripes. Repeat the colour sequence (order) when necessary.
4. Mount and display your work.

Activity 3

You will need:
adhesive paper in black and white
geometric templates
pencil, rubber, scissors

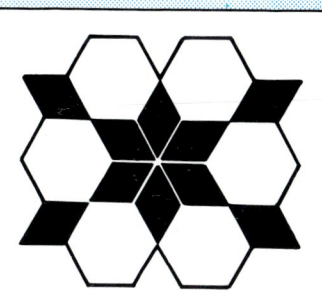

What to do
1. Using black and white paper only, design and make a collage based on geometric shapes. The overall size is to be 150 mm × 180 mm.
2. Mount and display your work.

Further work

1. What grouping of colours was discussed in 9.1? List this grouping.
2. Suggest other ways in which colours might be grouped. Give examples.
3. Suggest reasons why we tend to wear darker clothes in winter and lighter clothes in summer.
4. What colour is this van?

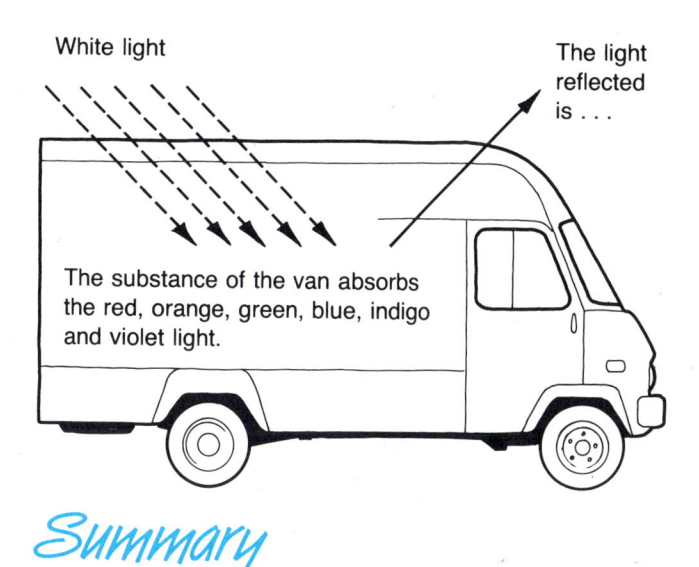

White light

The light reflected is . . .

The substance of the van absorbs the red, orange, green, blue, indigo and violet light.

Summary

The colours we see are the reflected parts of white light.

9.2 Fabrics and colour

You only need to look at the wealth of colourful fabrics available to realize that there are no **right** and **wrong** colours. It is your **individual preference** which makes you **choose** one fabric colour and design and **reject** another.
It is really very fortunate that everyone does not like the same thing. If this were so, fabric designers would have a much less interesting job.

Most fibres are a **neutral** colour (beige or cream) when they are first produced. If you think about it, you do not see coloured sheep in the fields unless they have just been dipped or marked with identification colours.

Whatever method of adding colour is chosen, the **dye** and the **fibre** must be **suitable** (compatible) as some dyes work better on certain fibres than others.
The dye must be **colour-fast** so that it does not 'run' or 'bleed' when in contact with water.
It must also stand up to the powerful **bleaching effect of sunlight** and it must not **fade**.

In order to '**fix**' the dye, a chemical called a **mordant** is used to bond the dye firmly to the fibre.

Hundreds of years ago the peasants wore **drab, natural coloured** clothes because this was the colour of the wool and skins they used. It was only the **wealthy** people who could afford to have their fabric **dyed** (coloured).
In those days the dyes used to colour fabric were made from **natural substances** found in **plants** and certain **animals** especially insects.
Ancient Britons used **woad**, a blue dye obtained from the woad plant, to decorate themselves.
A very expensive dye called **Tyrian purple** or **royal purple** was made from a species of Mediterranean whelk.
Saffron from the pollen of the autumn crocus produces a strong orange/yellow colour.
Nowadays most dyes are made from **chemicals**. The dye or colour can be added to the **fibre before it is spun** into yarn. The **yarn** itself can be dyed **before it is woven** or knitted into fabric. The colour may be applied to the **finished fabric before it is made up** into garments, etc.
Sometimes colour is applied **after the garment is completed**.

Things to do

9.2 Fabrics and colour

Some people still prefer to use dyes which are produced from **natural substances**. Such dyes often give **soft** and **subtle** colours.
In this investigation the **mordant** (fixing solution) used will be **tin mordant**.

Activity 1

Work in small groups.

Investigate the effectiveness of the dye on the fabric samples provided.

> You will need:
> apron or overall
> tin II chloride ⎫ mordant
> cream of tartar ⎭
> any natural plant substance, e.g. elderberries or blackberries
> undyed woollen fabric samples, e.g. old blanket (5 samples 50 mm × 50 mm)
> washing powder
> measuring jug
> scientific balance
> blender or liquidizer
> sieve
> 2 enamelled pans
> old wooden spoon
> 5 ml spoon
> iron and ironing board
> scissors

What to do

1. Make the dye
   (a) Put 30 g of berries into the liquidizer with a small amount of water. Liquidize them to a pulp.
   (b) Empty the pulp into the measuring jug. Add extra water to make the dye up to 500 ml.
   (c) Pour into a small saucepan and boil for 5 minutes.
   (d) Cool and strain into a clean saucepan (dye-bath).
2. Make the mordant
   (a) Put 500 ml of water in a jug. Dissolve 0.5 g of tin II chloride and 2 g of cream of tartar in the water.
   (b) Pour into a clean saucepan.
3. Investigate the effectiveness of the dye on the samples provided.
   (a) Put one fabric sample aside as a **control** which you can use to check what the original fabric was like.
   (b) Place two of the wool fabric samples in the mordant. Bring to the boil and simmer for ten minutes.
   (c) Remove the samples carefully with the wooden spoon. When cool, squeeze gently. Mark the samples by snipping so that you can identify them later.
   (d) Put these two samples and the two samples of fabric which have not been treated with the mordant into the dye-bath. Bring to the boil and simmer the samples for ten minutes.
   (e) Rinse all the samples under cold water and spin them in the spin drier to remove excess moisture.
   (f) Prepare two bowls of hand-hot water and put an equal amount of washing powder in each to make a lather.
   (g) Wash, rinse and spin dry one dyed sample which has been mordanted and one which has not.
   (h) Iron all your samples dry.
   (i) Compare your samples and complete the table below.

Dyed samples	Effect of dye	Effect of mordant on dye colour	Colour bleed on washing?	Effect of mordant on colour fastness
A				
B				
C				
D				

A, B fabric treated with mordant   C, D not treated with mordant

Further work

1. Use your school or local library to find pictures of historical costumes. Compare pictures of peasant costumes with pictures of the costumes of wealthy people of the same period.
2. Can you suggest reasons why royal purple was so named?
3. Find out about the ways in which colour is added to fabric.
4. Suggest another use for the dye, saffron.

Summary

The dye must be suitable for the fabric being dyed.

Fibres and fabrics

9.3 The business of dyeing

When you carried out the investigation using dyes in the previous unit you were probably quite happy with the colour you produced. You were not trying to make a **particular** colour or a certain **shade**.

Commercial dyeing is a much more complicated business than dyeing small items under home conditions.

So that he/she can meet the manufacturer's orders, the textile dyer must be able to produce a **specific** (accurate) colour. He/she must be able to **repeat** the colour **exactly** from one batch of dyeing to the next. The **same** colour may have to be produced on fabrics with a **different** fibre content, perhaps for coordinated outfits.

The colour that is produced must not **fade** in **sunlight**. It must be **colour-fast**.
Because commercial dyes are made from **chemicals**, the textile dyer must be certain that the fabric being dyed will not be **damaged** in any way.
Overcoming all these problems makes dyeing an **expensive** process which puts up the price of the finished fabric.

When a textile has been **completely immersed** (covered) in the dye the **depth** of the colour will be the **same** on both the front and the back of the fabric.

Sometimes colour is applied to (put on) **one** surface only. This process is called **printing**.

◆ Your teacher will show you samples of both processes.

By using a **variety** of dyeing and printing methods (techniques) textile designers can produce a very wide range of patterned textiles and colour combinations.

◆ Look carefully at the selection of fabric samples which your teacher has given you.

Use a hand lens and tweezers or a needle to help you decide at what stage of textile manufacture the **colour** was added.
By what method was the colour added?
Record your observations in a table.

Things to do

9.3 The business of dyeing

Activity 1

Work in small groups.

Investigate ways in which the technique of tie-dyeing can be varied to produce decorative effects.

Information

Tie-dyeing is a method of adding colour to fabric and creating attractive designs.

The fabric can be tied, folded, bound, knotted or sewn so that when it is immersed (put into) the dye-bath, colour does not penetrate (get into) some areas. The contrast of dyed and undyed areas forms interesting patterns and effects.

Special effects can be produced by tying marbles and buttons into the fabric.

You will need:
1 tin of shop-bought cold water dye
salt
washing soda
2 glass bowls
measuring jug
1 × 15 ml spoon
cotton or string
cotton fabric
apron or overall

What to do

1. Make the dye according to the instructions on the tin.
2. Wash, rinse and iron dry the cotton fabric.

◆ Can you suggest reasons why?

3. Tie up the sample as shown above to produce the effect you want.
4. Wet the sample and immerse in the dye for 30 minutes to 1 hour. Stir for the first 10 minutes.
5. Remove the fabric carefully from the dye-bath.
6. Wash the sample in hot water and rinse well.
7. Iron the sample dry. Display your work in a suitable way.

Further work

1. Write a few sentences to explain why dyeing is an expensive process.
2. Suggest reasons why most commercial dyes are made from chemicals.
3. Why is the fastness of the dye particularly important in these situations.

Summary

Colour can be applied to textiles at any stage of the manufacturing process.

Fibres and fabrics

9.4 Creating with colour

The **choice** of colour and pattern for clothes and furnishings is a matter of **personal preference**. However, most of us still have to choose from designs which represent the ideas of other people.

In this unit you are going to have the opportunity to **create** your own **colours** and **designs** on a piece of fabric.
Using a variety of **hand** and **machine** stitches you will then embroider your design to make an attractive picture or wall hanging.

Examples of creative textile work carried out in the needleskills department of Keldholme Comprehensive School, Middlesbrough

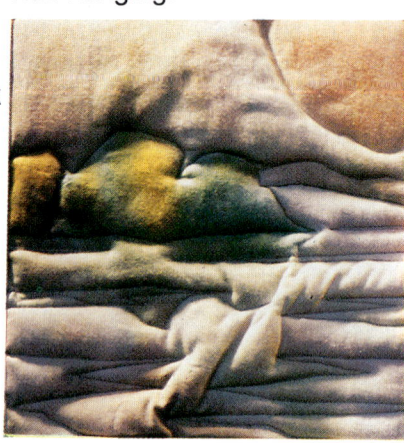

Billie-Jo Kershaw Age 13/14

Rajesh Mistry Age 13/14

Sean Yates Age 13/14

Paul Saunders Age 13/14

John Jordison Age 13/14

Lesley Crosby Age 13/14

You will need:

Step 1
drawing paper
pencil, rubber
coloured pencils

Step 2
white satin fabric 300 mm × 250 mm, ready washed and ironed dry
white backing fabric, e.g. curtain lining
wadding
commercial fabric paints, crayons or pastels
selection of paint brushes
blotting paper
drawing pins or clips
card for mounting

What to do

Step 1
1. Think about the theme of your design.
2. Think about a colour scheme.
3. Keeping your design fairly simple, draw it on to the drawing paper and colour it in.

Things to do

9.4 Creating with colour

Step 2

1. Place the sheet of blotting paper on a board or other flat surface.
2. Put the satin fabric over the blotting paper and secure it at the corners with drawing pins or clips.
3. Make up the shop-bought fabric paints or drawing inks according to the manufacturer's instructions.
4. Using your Step 1 drawing as a guide, paint your design on to the fabric. Do not worry if the colours merge at the edges.
5. It may be advisable to 'set' the design by ironing on the reverse side over the blotting paper. Read the manufacturer's instructions carefully.  
6. Place the backing material on a clean, flat surface.
7. Put the piece of wadding on top.
8. Place the painted fabric on top of the wadding.
9. Tack all three layers together carefully.
10. Set up the sewing machine and ask your teacher to check it.
11. Use the sewing machine and/or hand stitches to outline parts of your design.
12. Small details such as ladybirds, caterpillars or butterflies can be added using a variety of embroidery stitches.
13. Remove tackings.
14. Mount and display your work.

Further work

1. Using thin card, design shapes which could be stencilled on to fabric, paper or furniture. Draw diagrams to show how you would make the stencil shapes on the items.
2. Draw three finished designs for use on T shirts.

Summary

In order to satisfy our personal preferences we can experiment with colour and pattern.

Consumer awareness

10.1 Looking at advertising

Manufacturers are in business to make a **profit**. They will only make a profit if enough consumers (buyers) buy their products. There will be many **other** manufacturers making **similar** products, so how can we be persuaded to buy one brand rather than another?

Manufacturing companies spend a great deal of money on **advertising**. It is their way of **communicating** with the consumer. They may employ an **advertising agency** to work on **promoting** a particular product. The cost of this work will be passed on to the consumer in the price of the product.

Imagine that a new soap product has been developed. How might it be advertised? Promotional **leaflets, coupons** and **free samples** might be delivered to homes. **Posters** might be put up on hoardings. There might be **radio** and **television** advertising. The **cinema** might carry the advertisement and so might **magazines** and **newspapers**.

Advertising is about **persuading** people to part with their money in return for goods and services. In what ways does the advertiser set about trying to be persuasive?

The advertiser's aim is to make us **remember** the **name** of the manufacturer's particular **brand**.

Next time you watch a television programme on one of the commercial channels, try to notice how **frequently** the same advertisement is shown. Is the advertisement accompanied by a **catch-phrase** or a **jingle**?

Repetition of information is one way of making us remember. Catch-phrases and jingles are a means of making information stick in the memory.

Not all advertising is aimed at the same group of people. Advertisers try to reach as wide a **cross-section** of people as possible.

Some advertisements will be devised (planned) to appeal to the reader's **intelligence** and **reason**. Others are aimed at our **weaknesses**. Most of us care deeply about the **health** and **well-being** of our **family** and **friends** and are anxious to do our best for them.

◆ Find an advertisement which uses this anxiety as a means of persuading us to buy.

Many advertisers assume (think) that we would all like to be 'better' than we are: cleverer, slimmer, with a better lifestyle, better looking, browner, happier. Such advertisements are aimed at our **ambitions, desires** and **imagination**.

Remember though, that there are advertisements which give us **straightforward, factual** information.

Learn to recognize if an advertisement is **manipulating** (influencing) you in any way.

It is worth knowing that no matter how cleverly an advertiser puts over his/her message, he/she **must not make false statements**.

```
FOR SALE
Black Labrador puppies.
4 dogs, 2 bitches. 10 wks. old.
K.C. reg. Inoculated.
£85 each.

Phone 697421 after 6 p.m.
```

Things to do

10.1 Looking at advertising

Activity 1

Work in small groups.

> You will need:
> selection of magazines, colour supplements, newspapers
> scissors
> thin card
> glue

What to do

1. Look through the magazines and newspapers for a wide variety of advertisements for different products.
2. Cut out the advertisements and mount them on thin card.
3. Number each advertisement for identification.
4. Compare the advertisements and discuss with the class the way in which the advertiser has used **language, creative skills** and **advertising technique** to put across his/her message.
5. Study and group (classify) the advertisements as follows:
   (a) those which give **factual** information only
   (b) those which are intended to appeal to people's
       (i) **emotions**   (ii) **desires**
       (iii) **appetites**   (iv) **ambitions**
       (v) **imagination**
   (c) those which enable you to make an **informed choice** about the product.

Activity 2

Work in small groups.

> You will need:
> drawing paper
> pencil, rubber, ruler
> coloured pencils or paints

Your school plans to raise money for charity by holding a Summer Fair.

1. Design two **contrasting** posters advertising an event to be held at the Fair using some of the techniques discussed in Unit 10.1. Remember that you must not make any **false claims**.
2. Display your work and join with other groups to discuss the impact (effect) of the posters.

Further work

1. Suggest a situation in which advertising might help to reduce the cost of a product.
2. Which people would you consider to be particularly at risk from clever advertising? Give reasons for your answers.
3. What is the name of the authority which sets out a code of practice for advertisers?
4. If you felt that an advertiser was making dishonest claims, whom would you contact?

Summary

Advertisers must not make false claims.

10.2 Looking at packaging

Only a matter of a few decades ago the majority of goods in a grocer's shop were sold 'loose' and were only wrapped at the **point of sale**. Butter stood on marble slabs in keg-shaped mounds.
Dried fruits were scooped from wooden boxes. Sugar was sold in plain blue paper bags and soap was wrapped in newspaper.

Nowadays much **time, thought** and **money** is spent by manufacturers in designing packaging which is **colourful** and **eye-catching**. After all, it is **their** product that they want us to buy. Fortunately for the consumer (buyer), packaging has many **valuable** uses other than being yet another way in which the manufacturer **persuades** us to buy his/her product.

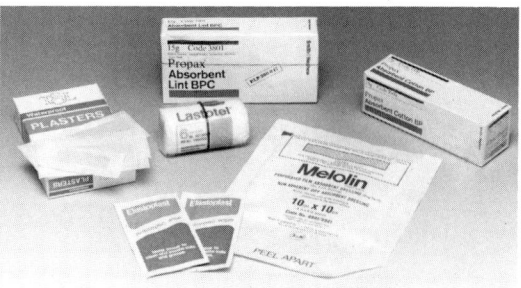

Packaging helps to keep the contents **clean** and protected from flies, dust, soiled hands and micro-organisms.

Well-designed packaging can **protect** the contents from **damage**.

Suitable packaging can prevent variations in **weather conditions** (climate) having a harmful effect on foodstuffs.

Some **perishable foods** can be displayed pre-packed in **clean, hygienic** containers which can be **disposable** or **returnable**.

Packaging designs have become so attractive and functional (useful) that many items are now **bought** and **stored** in the same container.

Many shops are well aware that attractive packaging **improves the image** of a product and offer a gift-wrapping service for purchases which are going to be given as presents.

The **informed** and **careful** consumer (buyer) knows how to get much useful information from the labels on packages. These labels give information on safety, performance, care and contents. See Book 1, Unit 10.

Things to do

10.2 Looking at packaging

Activity 1

Local shop or supermarket survey

Work in a small group or with a partner.

Your teacher will make arrangements for you to visit your local shop or supermarket.
1. Look carefully at the ways in which goods for sale are packaged and displayed.
2. Suggest a classification (grouping) for each different type of packaging.
3. Select six items which are packaged differently and study their packaging using the following headings.

Brand name	Classification (type of packaging)	Aesthetic appeal (Does the packaging look attractive?)	Suitability for contents	Useful consumer information on package	Could the cost of the packaging be reduced without affecting the contents? How?	Additional comments

4. Discuss the results of your survey with the other groups.

Activity 2

Work on your own.

Presents do not have to be expensive in order to give pleasure. Often care and thought in packaging can increase the pleasure of the person who receives the present.

Practise 'gift-wrapping' a small package to make it look attractive. At the same time keep the packaging costs as low as possible.

Further work

1. Write a few sentences to explain the value of packaging from
    (a) the manufacturer's (seller's) point of view
    (b) the consumer's (buyer's) point of view.
2. Suggest ways in which manufacturers sometimes disguise changes in the contents by clever use of packaging.
3. Explain the term 'point of sale'.
4. Collect examples of informative and misleading packaging for a class display.
5. Which packet opposite represents best value for money? Why?

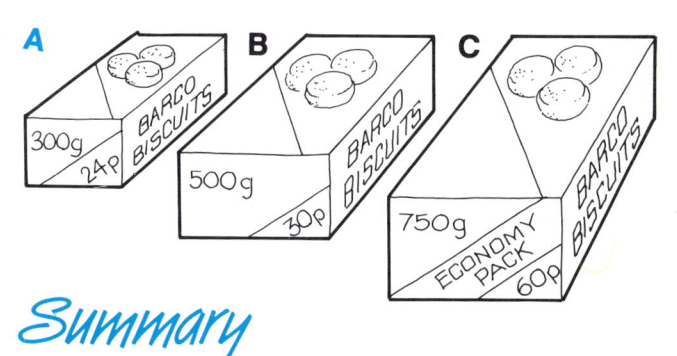

Summary

Learn to tell the difference between informative and misleading packaging.

Consumer awareness

10.3 Shops

Look carefully at the picture opposite and the diagram below.
Consider (think about) the **limited choices** available in the past when people **exchanged** and **bartered** goods with passers-by.
Now consider the **wide range** of retail outlets (shops) available to us.

◆ Is a wide range of choice an advantage?

◆ Do you think that too many decisions have to be made?

◆ Discuss your feelings about choice with the rest of your class.

◆ List the advantages of having a wide choice of retail outlets.

◆ Is any one retail outlet better than another?

RETAIL OUTLETS
- Market stall
- Door to door selling
- Department store
- Mail order
- Hypermarket
- Supermarket
- Corner shop
- Direct selling
- Mobile van
- Chain store
- Specialist shop

You will probably have realized that there are no hard and fast rules. One type of retail outlet will suit someone in a particular situation but will not suit everyone.

◆ Look carefully at the scenes pictured below. Suggest, with reasons, which retail outlet(s) would suit each set of circumstances.

Things to do

10.3 Shops

Activity 1

Work with a partner or in a small group.

Many attractive items available in the shops can be made at home. Carry out an investigation to compare the cost of a home-made item with that of a similar one bought from a retail outlet (shop).

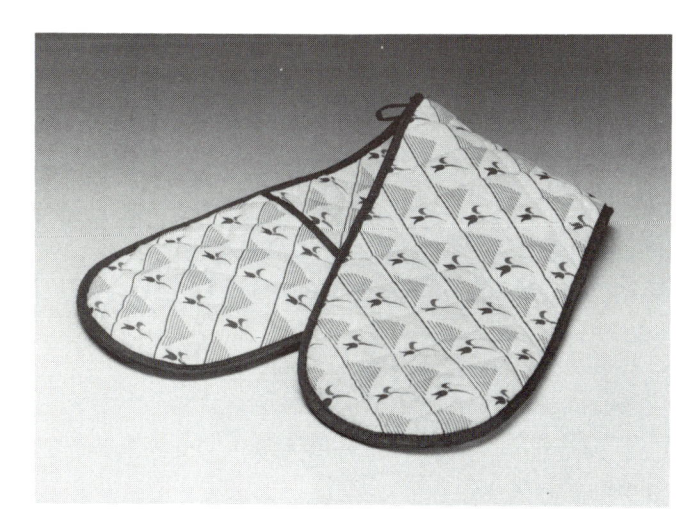

You will need:
squared drawing paper, pencil, ruler, rubber
selection of fabrics and textiles with composition and price per metre clearly marked
selection of insulating materials with price per metre
sewing equipment, priced where appropriate
sewing machine

◆ Here is a simply designed oven glove.

Study the design features.
What fabric is it made from?
Why is it suitable for the job it performs?
How is it made?
What additional notions (thread, bias binding, etc.) will you need to make a similar item?
What care instructions are there?
What 'hidden' factors add to the cost of the article?

What to do

Once you start, keep a check on the time you spend on this activity.

1. Design an oven glove using the bought item as a guide.
2. Draw out the pattern on the squared paper.
3. Select suitable fabrics and materials to make the oven glove.
4. Cut out the oven glove and make a careful note of the amounts of all fabrics, etc. used.
5. Make up the oven glove.
6. Carefully work out the cost of the materials for making the oven glove.
7. Suggest a list of care instructions.
8. Display your work. Discuss the work of all the groups.

Complete this table.

Article to be made	Amount of fabric(s) used	Cost of all fabrics/materials used	Time spent on (a) designing (b) making article	Cost of time per hour	Hidden costs, e.g. premises, heating, lighting, power	Realistic price of home-made article	Shop price of similar article

Further work

1. Account for the difference in price between the shop-bought and home-made article.
2. Use your knowledge of advertising techniques to design and make a poster which shows that your class has oven gloves or other articles for sale.
3. What points did you take into account when fixing the price for the home-made article?
4. Are there any changes you could make which would allow the finished article to be priced more competitively?

Summary

Having a wide choice of retail outlets involves us in many decisions.

Consumer awareness

10.4 Shopping

Perhaps your family has a garden or an allotment where you can grow fruit and vegetables. It is difficult to judge just how much to plant, and often there is a bigger crop than you really need. A neighbour's hens might be laying well and producing more eggs than he/she can use. It seems sensible to **exchange** (swap) **surplus** (extra) products so that each person **benefits**.

It was in a similar way that **trade** first started. People **bartered** (swapped) surplus goods. Gradually they found it more **convenient** to **buy** the things they wanted with shells, ornaments and beads.

Round about 500 BC **coins** came into use. The coins were made of **metal** and the **value of the metal used** was stamped on to the coin's surface.

Today coins are only **symbols** or **tokens** of worth and their value is only **face-value**.

We spend our money on a wide range of **goods** and **services**.

This country produces a wide variety of **manufactured** goods. Some remain in this country but **surplus** goods are sold abroad (**exported**).

There are **commodities** (goods) which are made much more **cheaply** abroad as well as **foodstuffs** which do not grow in this country. These goods have to be **imported**.

Through **trade**, countries try to **balance** the **export** and **import** of goods.

In much the same way that countries need to maintain (keep) a **balance of trade** to prevent financial (money) problems, so *we* have to learn to handle our money sensibly.

In the shops we are faced with a wide choice of **attractive** goods and are bombarded with **advertisements** and **incentives** (free gifts, coupons) to make us part with our money.

If we are in the habit of going round the shops as a means of passing the time, we are likely to be **tempted** to buy the items on display. This kind of buying is called **impulse buying**. It is buying which takes place on the spur of the moment without stopping to consider if the purchase is **really needed** or if it is **good value for money**.

On the other hand, you may have been thinking for some time that you need a new item of clothing or some new equipment. You will have had a chance to look **carefully** at the **available choices**. You might have looked in several shops to check **quality** and **prices**. You might have studied **consumer magazines** to compare **performances**. You might also have considered which shops have a **good reputation** for **quality** and for **reliable** service.

This kind of buying is called **considered** or **planned buying**.

Things to do

10.4 Shopping

Activity 1

Study the situations below.

On the spur of the moment Rosemary went into the pet shop and bought the kitten.

1 What feelings prompted Rosemary to buy the kitten?
2 What problems might Rosemary have now that the kitten is hers?
3 What would you consider to have been sensible action in this situation?

Basil has been planning to buy some hi-fi equipment. He has been saving regularly for several months.

Make a list of all the points Basil has had time to consider before making the purchase.

Here the Smith family is out doing the shopping. Mrs Smith is selecting items as she sees them. The children are doing the same.

1 Do you consider that this is a sensible way for the Smiths to do the shopping?
2 What will be the likely outcome (result) of this type of shopping?
3 If Mrs Smith wanted advice on a more sensible way to shop, what would you suggest?

Further work

1 Explain the difference between impulse buying and considered (planned) buying.
2 Use your school or local library to find out how markets and shops developed in the Middle Ages.
3 In January 1973 Britain joined the European Economic Community (EEC). On an outline map of Europe shade in or colour the countries which now belong to the EEC.
4 What are the trading advantages for countries belonging to the EEC?
5 Collect a selection of logos or trademarks.
   (a) Identify the country of origin from these trademarks.
   (b) List the countries which have the benefit of free trade with Britain.
   (c) Which countries' goods will carry import duty when they come into Britain?

Summary

Try to plan your spending.
Avoid buying on impulse.

Unit 1   Recap

How is the body kept warm?
The foods we eat help to keep the body warm through the release of **energy**.

The body can produce warmth by **shivering** ...

The **sun** on the body produces warmth.

... or by strenuous **exercise**.

In colder climates we need the protection of **extra clothing** to keep warm.

How is the home heated?
The main source of heat comes from the **heating system** of the house, e.g. central heating.
The **Sun's rays** warm up the fabric of the house by heating the walls and the roof.
Sunshine gets into the house through the windows and through special solar panels.
When we cook food, heat from the **cooker** escapes into the house.
Hot water pipes carry water around the house. Unless they are well lagged some heat escapes.
The **people** in the house warm it with their body heat.
Electric light bulbs give off heat energy as well as light energy.

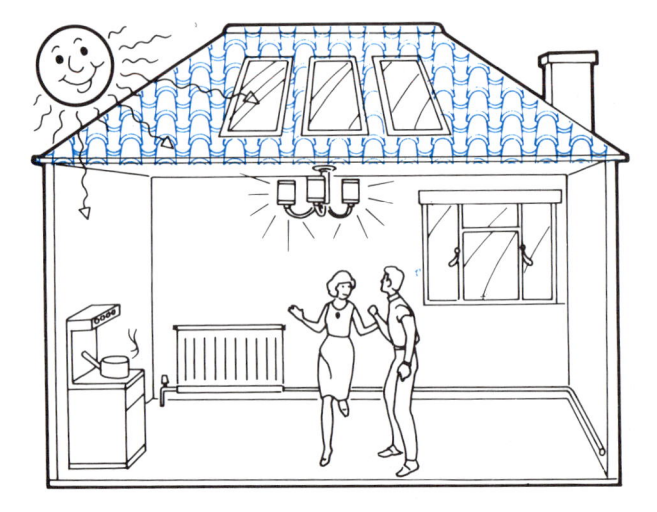

How is heat lost in an uninsulated house?
Suggest ways in which heat loss in the home can be reduced:
(a) roof
(b) cavity walls
(c) windows
(d) draughts and ventilation
(e) floors.

Unit 2 Recap

One of the nice things about having **relatives** and **friends** is that you can invite them to your **home**. Extended families tend to gather together on **special occasions**, often at weddings, funerals and child-naming ceremonies or to celebrate a variety of **religious festivals**.

Wedding

Child-naming ceremony

Bar mitzvah

In the normal way friends will **call round** or **ring up** when they want to see you. They do not feel that they need a **special invitation**.

However, there will be times when you **invite** friends to your home, perhaps to celebrate a birthday or to **share each other's company** for some other reason. No matter how **informal** the gathering, as the **host** or **hostess** you have certain **duties** and **courtesies** to perform for your guests.

It's a good idea to know in advance that all the guests are likely to get along with each other. It is your job to make them feel **welcome** when they arrive, to put them **at ease** and to make sure that **everyone knows who everyone else is**. Keep a sharp eye open to make sure that **no-one** is being **left out** of whatever is going on.

◆ Make a checklist of points which you think a good host or hostess should consider if giving a party for
(a) friends of his/her own age
(b) friends and relatives of mixed ages.

Unit 3 Recap

You live in Beeston, Nottingham. You have friends and relatives who live locally and around the country.
Work out the cost of the following telephone calls.

You will need:
a map of Great Britain
a ruler
telephone dialling code book

Mon	Tue	Wed	Thur	Fri	Sat	Sun
Cheap rate		6.00pm–8.00am				
Standard rate		8.00am–9.00am				Cheap Rate All Day
Peak rate		9.00am–1.00pm				
Standard rate		1.00pm–6.00pm				

1. Your aunt Amelia who lives in Exeter is a hopeless chatterbox. As it is her birthday you want to 'phone her with birthday greetings. Which will be the most economical time of the day to make the telephone call?
How much will it cost for a conversation lasting two minutes?

2. Basil likes to chat to his friend Debbie who lives round the corner. Yesterday lunch time at 12.30 he talked to Debbie for ten minutes. How much did the call cost?
How much less would it have cost to phone her at 18.15 for the same length of time?

3. Your mother's best friend lives in Derby. As she does not have a telephone of her own, she arranges to receive calls during her lunch break (12.00 to 13.00) at work.
Your mother knows that she pays £1.16 for the telephone call.
How long was your mother able to speak with her friend?

Dialled Calls Local				Approximate **Cost** to the customer including VAT					Time for one unit
				1 min	2 mins	3 mins	4 mins	5 mins	
Local	L		Cheap	6p	6p	6p	6p	6p	8 mins
			Standard	6p	6p	12p	12p	17p	2 mins
			Peak	6p	12p	12p	17p	23p	1 min 30 secs
National									
Calls up to 56 km (35 miles)	a		Cheap	6p	6p	12p	12p	17p	2 mins
			Standard	12p	17p	29p	35p	46p	40 secs
			Peak	12p	23p	35p	46p	58p	30 secs
Calls over 56 km (35 miles) connected over low cost routes	b1		Cheap	6p	12p	17p	23p	29p	1 min
			Standard	12p	23p	35p	46p	58p	30 secs
			Peak	17p	35p	46p	63p	81p	22.5 secs
Calls over 56 km (35 miles)	b		Cheap	12p	17p	23p	29p	40p	48 secs
			Standard	17p	35p	46p	63p	81p	22.5 secs
			Peak	23p	40p	63p	81p	£1.04	17.1 secs

Unit 4 Recap

1 When a knight took part in a jousting contest he knew the advantages of protective clothing.

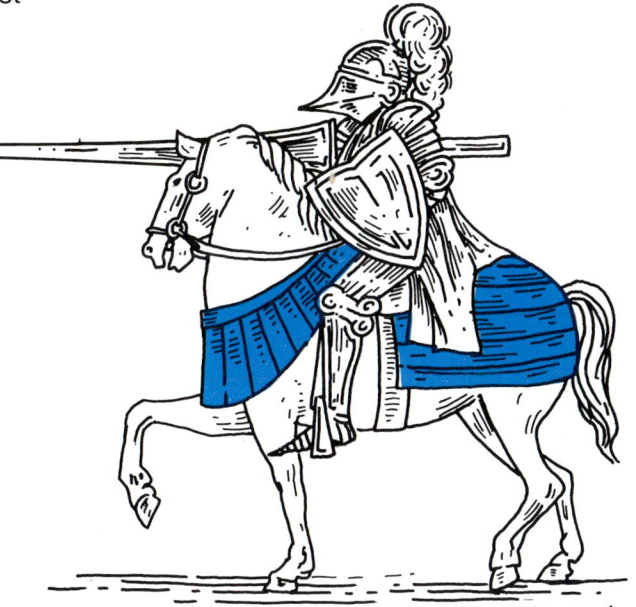

Suggest what protective clothing each of these people will need in order to do their work without harming themselves or other people. Give reasons for your answers.

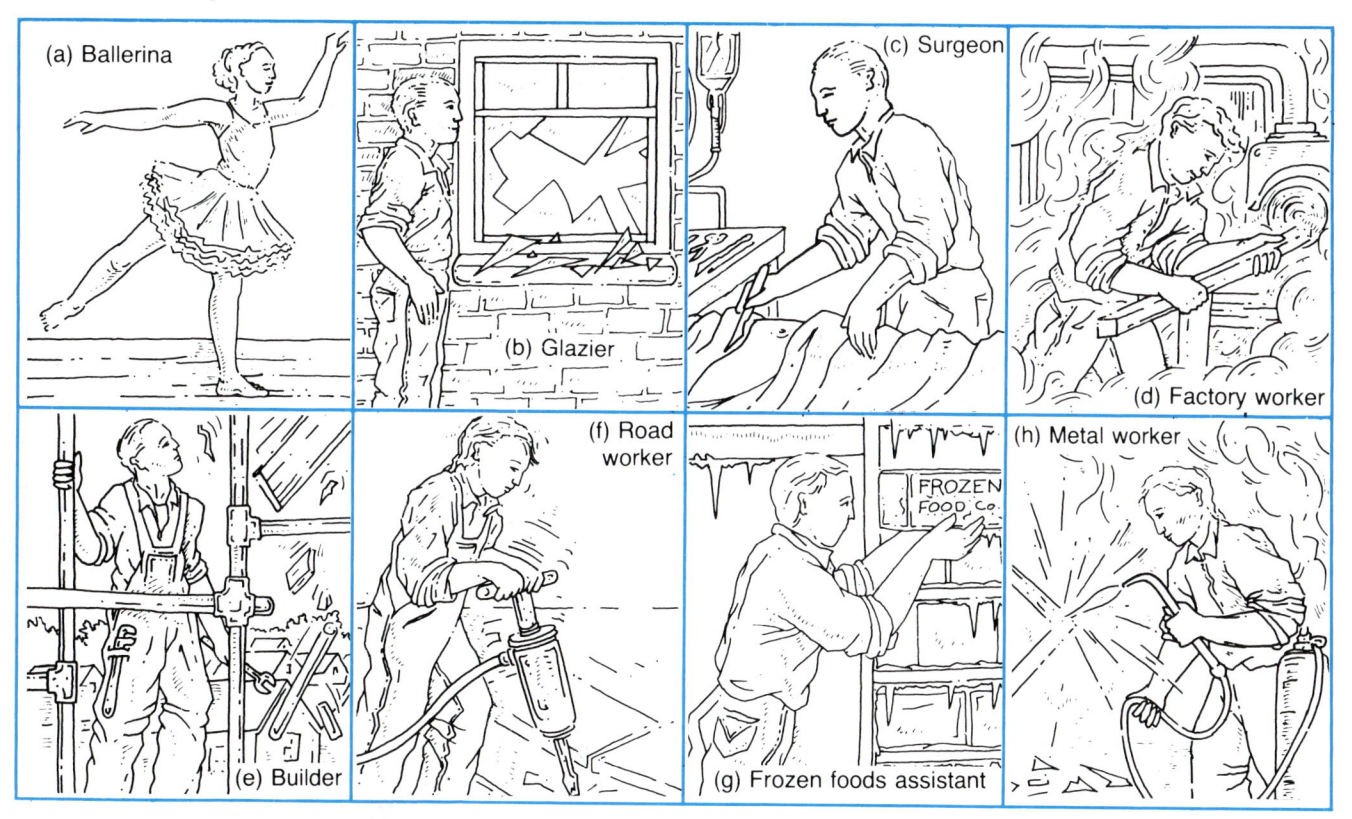

(a) Ballerina
(b) Glazier
(c) Surgeon
(d) Factory worker
(e) Builder
(f) Road worker
(g) Frozen foods assistant
(h) Metal worker

1 Nowadays more and more sportsmen and women are wearing protective clothing to limit injury. Suggest what protective clothing the following sportspeople might need:
(a) boxer
(b) weightlifter
(c) sprinter
(d) mountaineer
(e) fencer
(f) speed cyclist
(g) American footballer
(h) hockey player
(i) cricketer

Unit 5 Recap

Recent medical reports from NACNE, COMA and JACNE suggest ways in which we can take **positive** steps to develop **healthier eating habits**.

◆ Why do you think these independent medical committees are concerned about the British diet?

These reports advise us that, in order to develop a healthier lifestyle and to try to avoid diseases and conditions linked to poor diet, we must:

Cut down on sugar
Too much sugar causes tooth decay and can lead to obesity (being overweight).

> JACNE
> (Joint Advisory Committee on Nutrition Education)
>
> NACNE
> (National Advisory Committee on Nutrition Education)
>
> COMA
> (Committee on the Medical Aspects of Food Policy)

Cut down on salt
Too much salt can lead to high blood pressure and heart problems.

Cut down on fats
Too much fat may lead to weight and heart problems.

Eat more fibre
Fibre helps digestion and speeds up the passage of food through the digestive system.

Many **responsible** food retail outlets are trying to make it **easier** for customers to **identify** foods which contribute to a **healthy, balanced diet**.

◆ Next time you are in your local supermarket, make a point of asking for literature which gives guidance about healthy eating.

Remember that **healthy eating** depends on having the right **balance** of foodstuffs from a **wide variety** of foods.

◆ Suggest ways in which your family could try to meet the dietary guidelines set out in the reports.

◆ Is healthy eating alone sufficient to ensure a healthy lifestyle?

Unit 6 Recap

Are you a responsible babysitter?
Many teenage boys and girls earn a little pocket-money from babysitting jobs.
Whether you act as a babysitter **occasionally** or **often**, for **friends, relatives** or **acquaintances**, the job carries a lot of **responsibility**.

In asking you to take charge, the parents are expecting you to be **responsible** for their child's **safety**. The parents are placing a certain amount of **trust** and **confidence** in you.

◆ Read this story.

Phil's mum met Maureen in the butcher's shop. Maureen was going out that evening and needed a babysitter for her baby son, Matthew. Maureen did not know Phil very well but when his mother said that Phil would babysit, Maureen accepted thankfully.

Phil was not too pleased at this arrangement. He had intended to play football with his friends that evening.

When he arrived at Maureen's house he was in a bad mood. Maureen took one glance at him and dashed out, shouting that if he wanted anything for his supper he was to look in the fridge.

No sooner had Maureen slammed the door than Matthew started to scream. When Phil went upstairs to find out what was the matter, Matthew only screamed louder. Phil thought the baby looked very hot and rather spotty. As he was not sure what babies should look like, he closed the bedroom door and went back downstairs.

The prospect of an evening with a screaming baby didn't appeal to Phil. He decided to ring up two of his pals to come and help him pass the time. In the meantime the best thing seemed to be to play some music very loudly indeed!

Make a list of all the mistakes Maureen, Phil and his mother made.

◆ If you were asked to babysit, what information would you want from the child's parents before you agreed to the arrangement?

◆ Devise (work out) an 'Information Card' which would be useful to any teenager doing a baby-sitting job.

Unit 7 Recap

When you buy a piece of electrical equipment you often need to fit a plug on to it. The skills involved in carrying out this task are quite straightforward as long as you understand what you are doing. Practise carrying out this task. Ask your teacher to check your work.

You will need:
small screwdriver
wire stripper or sharp scissors

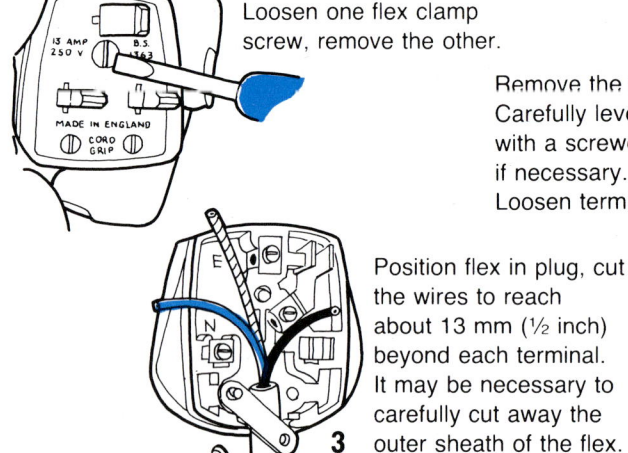

1 Unscrew the plug cover. Loosen one flex clamp screw, remove the other.

2 Remove the fuse. Carefully lever it out with a screwdriver if necessary. Loosen terminal screws.

3 Position flex in plug, cut the wires to reach about 13 mm (½ inch) beyond each terminal. It may be necessary to carefully cut away the outer sheath of the flex.

4 Carefully strip enough insulation to expose about 6 mm (¼ inch) of wire for screwhole terminals, about 13 mm (½ inch) for clamp type ones.
Take care not to cut any strands of wire. Twist the strands of each wire together.

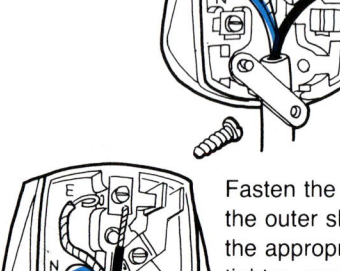

5a Fasten the cable clamp firmly over the outer sheath. Fit each wire into the appropriate terminal hole and tighten each screw. Check that there are no stray 'whiskers' of bare wire.
NB: If the wires are small it may help to fold them over and then put them into the terminal holes.

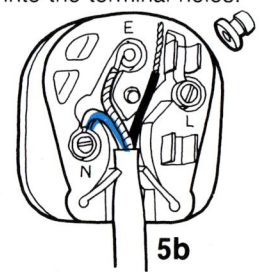

5b

For clamp type terminals:
Wrap wire clockwise around the pillar. Tighten screw.

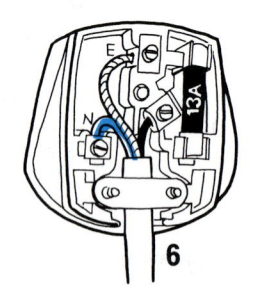

6

Finally check:
1 wires are connected to the correct terminals
2 there are no stray 'whiskers' of wire
3 flex clamp is on outer sheath of cable, not on wires
4 all screws are tight.

Then:
5 fit the correct fuse.
6 refit plug cover and screw tight.

Remember:
▨ Green/yellow wire to Earth terminal (marked E or ⏚)
▬ Blue wire to Neutral terminal (marked N)
▬ Brown wire to Live terminal (marked L)
Two core flex (live and neutral only) is used for double insulated appliances not needing an earth.

Warning If you are in any doubt whatsoever when wiring plugs or replacing fuses, stop what you are doing and get expert advice.

Unit 8 Recap

Design solutions to these problems.
Have fun! You will have to try this one out to solve the problem.

1. The cork has fallen into the wine bottle. Find a way of removing the cork intact without breaking the bottle.

2. Five friends went off to the seaside for the day. When it was time to return they found they had missed the bus home. They decided to look around for other means of transport. All they could come up with was a donkey, a camel, a pedal car, a skateboard and a motor-cycle. Alan was the only one legally allowed to ride a motor-cycle. Basil couldn't even stand up on the skateboard. Colin had been on holiday in Morocco and said that he knew how to ride a camel. Rosemary said that she did not mind what she had as long as she could get home. Debbie said that she thought she could manage the pedal car.
When they had sorted themselves out the friends set off.

   ◆ Who had the donkey, the camel, the pedal car, the skateboard and the motor-cycle?

3. The following ingredients are available to you.

   > 6 lemons
   > 225 g polyunsaturated margarine
   > 25 g polyunsaturated white fat
   > 200 g caster sugar
   > 275 g granulated sugar
   > 6 eggs
   > 100 g SR flour
   > 100 g plain flour
   > 25 g cornflour

   The theme of your cooking is 'Lemons'. From the ingredients listed 'make' as many dishes as you can. Aim to use up as many of the ingredients as possible.
   You may use water and salt as necessary. Use a basic recipe book or recipe file to help you.

Unit 9   Recap

Use your knowledge of design, use of colour and textile fibres to create an attractive needlework picture. Choose a subject which interests you.

Step 1
If possible take a photograph of your chosen subject or use one from a magazine or book. Study the photograph carefully and make a detailed drawing to highlight interesting features.

You will need:
photocopy of canvas mesh
white needlepoint canvas (6 meshes to the cm)
selection of coloured 2-ply yarns
tapestry needle, scissors
drawing paper
ruler, pencil, rubber

Step 2
Your teacher will give you a photocopy of the mesh of your canvas. Transfer the drawing of your design on to the canvas photocopy. Take care that you draw **between** the lines of the canvas mesh and not on them. Make sure that the final drawing looks **balanced** and that the **proportions** are accurate.

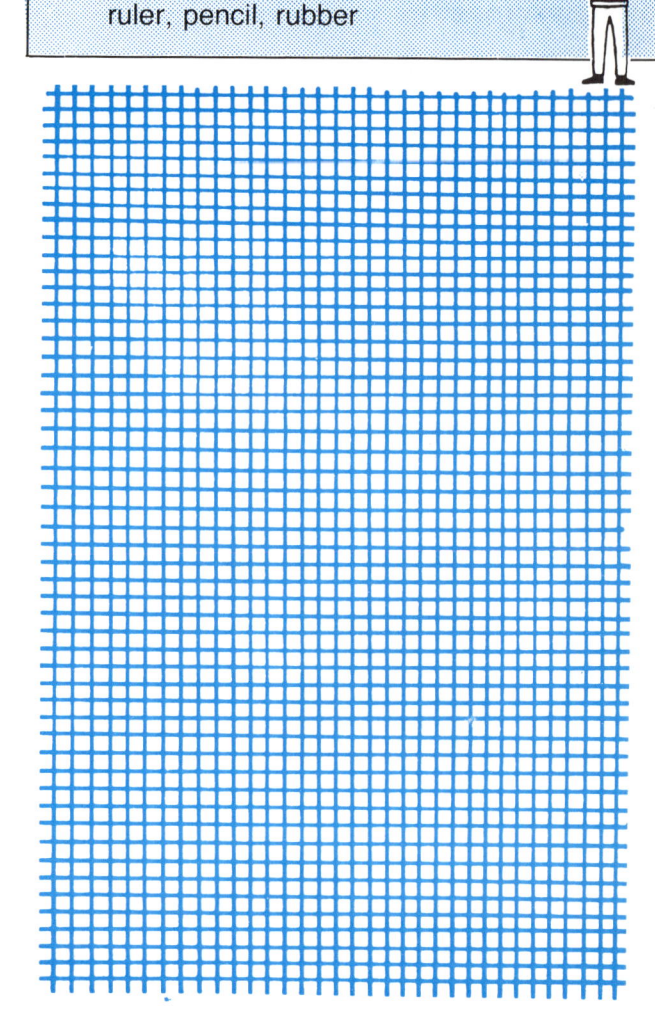

Step 3
Use books which show a wide range of stitches suitable for canvas work.
Select and practise using stitches which will enhance the **detail** in your design.

Step 4
Use a combination of different canvas stitches, worked in carefully chosen colours or mixtures of colours (2 × 2 ply strands of yarn).
Take care to create **textures** and **details** which will make your design **individual**.

Step 5
Your finished design could be mounted as a picture or used as a decorative panel on a stool, cushion or bag.

Unit 10   Recap

Twice a year, round about January and July, many retail outlets throughout the country advertise the start of the 'Sales'.

Why do shops hold Sales?

The main idea is to **get rid** of all the goods which have **not sold well** and to **make room** for the **new season's** merchandise.

A late spring and wet start to summer can spell disaster for fashion departments. People are unwilling to buy clothes for a summer that looks as though it will never begin.

A typical **Sales gimmick** is to display a **loss-leader** in the shop window. A loss-leader is an item which is priced well **below** its value so that it **attracts the attention** of the public. It does **not** mean that all the other merchandise in the store is also underpriced or such an obvious bargain.

For the **wise** shopper there may well be bargains. He/she will have checked and compared **prices, quality** and **after sales service**. The wise shopper will know exactly what he/she wants to buy and how much money is available to spend on it.

It is the **impulsive** shopper who is at risk at Sales time.

A shopper who goes to the Sales with no clear idea of **what he/she wants** will not know if an item is really **needed** and will not have much idea of its **real value**. This person is likely to make **expensive** mistakes.

◆ Think up several questions for the impulsive shopper to ask him/herself before going to the Sales.

Glossary

Absorb: take in 5.4
Abuse: use wrongly 2.4, 6.4
Advanced society: well developed society 4.4
Advertising agency: where advertisements are created 10.1
Aesthetic: concerning beauty 8.1, 10.2
Aggression: hostility 6.2
Alphabetical order: a, b, c, d, e, etc. 3.3
Alternative: other choice 1.3
Ambition: desire for success 10.1
Ancestor: person from whom family descent can be traced 3.1
Anthropometrics: study of body size and movement 8.2
Anus: body opening through which solid waste matter is passed 5.4
Appetite: desire for food 5.3
Appropriate: suitable 3.2
Arthritis: painful inflammation of the joints 8.2
Automatic: working without human control 6.3

Bachelor: unmarried man 3.1
Balance of trade: balancing goods imported with goods exported 10.4
Barter: trade goods for goods 10.3, 10.4
Behaviour pattern: usual way of responding 3.2
'Bleed': run (of dye) 9.2
Body language: communication suggested by body movement 2.2
Bonded: not woven 1.1
Book stock: range of books in a library 3.3
Building site: where building work is done 3.4
Built-in oven: oven fitted either above or below the working surface 7.2
Bully: to hurt a weaker person 6.2

Catalogue: file or list of books in a library 3.3
Catch-phrase: phrase which is easily learnt and recalled 10.1
Century: one hundred years 1.4
Ceramic: toughened glass 7.1
Chlorine: chemical used to purify water 4.1
Circulation: circular movement 5.4
Clock meter: meter with clock dial marked 1–10 1.4
Coast: seaside 1.1
Coat of arms: shield decorated with symbolic designs 2.3
Code of practice: guidelines (for advertising) 10.1
Colour-fast: will not shed colour in water 9.2, 9.3
Colour scheme: choice of colours for room decoration 8.3
Colour supplement: magazine section of a newspaper 10.1
Compassion: feeling of understanding 2.4
Compile: collect and put together 3.4
Commodities: goods 10.4
Communication: passing on or sharing news and information 2.2
Concentrated: strong 8.4
Condense: change into a liquid from a gas 4.1
Conduction: heat energy transferred through or along a body 5.2
Confide: trust with a secret 2.1
Confidence: trust in oneself or another person 6.2, 6.4

Considered buying: buying something when you have thought carefully about it 10.4
Consumer: user or customer 10.1
Contaminate: pollute or make impure 4.1, 4.2
Convection: transfer of heat in liquid or gas 5.2, 7.3
Conventional: operates in the usual way 7.3
Corrosion: gradual eating away 8.1
Cross-section: sample 10.1
Cubic foot: a measurement by volume of gas 1.4
Cultural: relating to the beliefs and customs of a society 2.3

Decade: ten years 1.4, 10.2
Decay: rot away 5.3, 8.1
Decibel: unit of sound intensity 4.4
Degree: unit of temperature 1.4
Dependent: relying on another for care and support 2.2
Deteriorate: become worse 5.1
Dewey decimal classification: system used in a library for grouping information according to subject 3.3
Dietary fibre: indigestible cellulose 5.4
Digital meter: meter which gives information as digits 1.4
Discolour: change colour 5.1
Dispose: get rid of 4.2
Draught excluder: device to stop draughts 1.4
Dual circuit: two circuits 7.1, 7.2

Economical: avoiding waste and expense 1.4
Edible: can be eaten 5.3
Emotion: strong feeling 2.2, 8.3
Employee: person who works for a company or organization 3.4
Environment: surrounding area 4.4
Enzyme: chemical which makes a reaction happen faster 5.1
Excess: extra 5.1
Exchange: give and receive 10.3, 10.4
Exhausted: used up 1.4
Export: send goods to another country 10.4
Eye-catching: attracting attention 5.3

Fabric softener: liquid added to final rinse to soften fabrics 8.4
Face-value: value stated on something 10.4
Factual: something which has really happened 10.1
Fade: lose intensity of colour 9.2, 9.3
Fan-assisted (electric oven): oven where the heat is circulated by a fan 7.3
Feelings: emotions 8.3
Flow-chart: step-by-step sequence 1.2
Flex: to bend 8.1
Food energy: energy supplied to the body by food 1.3
Fossil fuel: fuel formed from long-dead plants and animals 1.3
Free-standing cooker: cooker which is not built-in or under a work surface 7.1
Friendship: friendly relationship 2.1
Functional: something which works 10.2

Garnish: to decorate, usually with something savoury 7.2
Gauze plate: heating element in a grill made of metal woven into a 'net' 7.2
Geothermal (energy): from rocks 1.3

Good conductor: good carrier (of electricity) 5.2
Gregarious: living in groups 2.3
Grill frets: heating component in a grill which is made of criss-crossed metal strips 7.2

Harness: to control something so it can be used 1.3
Hazard: source of danger 3.1, 3.4
Heat energy: energy in the form of heat 1.3, 5.2
Heat-proof: resistant to heat 8.1
Heat zones: areas with different temperatures in an oven 7.3
Heating element: source of heat 7.3
Hidden costs: costs which add to the price of an article but which are not immediately obvious 10.3
Hob: part of the cooker on which pans are placed 7.1, 7.2
Holiday resort: popular place for a holiday 3.1
Hot water cylinder: tank to hold domestic hot water 1.4
Household: all the people of a house or home 4.1
Hydro-electric power: electricity produced from water 1.3
Hypothermia: abnormally low body temperature 3.1, 4.4

Image: the way a product appears 10.2
Imagination: creative thinking 6.1
Immerse: put something in a liquid so it is completely covered 9.2, 9.3
Impair: to spoil 8.2
Impermeable: cannot be passed through 4.1
Import: to bring in from outside (the country) 10.4
Import duty: tax on goods coming into the country 10.4
Impulse buying: buying without sufficient thought 10.4
Incentive: something which encourages us to do something 10.4
Income: total money received 1.1
Independence: ability to operate alone 6.2
Index: alphabetical list of contents 3.3
Inedible: cannot be eaten 5.1
Influence: to have an effect on 6.2
Informed choice: choice as a result of research 10.1
Inhibit: restrain or hinder 4.2
Insecure: unsafe 6.2
Insulate: cover with non heat-conducting material to prevent heat-loss 1.4, 7.3
Insulator: something which does not allow electricity to pass through it 5.2
Intellect: the ability of the mind to reason 6..
Intellectual growth: development of the ability to reason 2.2

Jealousy: resentful or suspicious attitude to someone's success 2.1
Jingle: catchy tune 10.1

Key word: important word 3.1

Lagging jacket: covering used to insulate the hot water cylinder 5.2
Leisure activities: activities carried out in free time 2.3
Lifestyle: way of living 1.1
Light energy: energy in the form of light 1.3
Local authority: locally elected council 4.1
Lock stitch: straight stitch 7.4
Logo: symbol associated with one company or brand of product 10.4
Loyal: always on your side 2.1

Micro-organism: very small living creature 4.2, 5.1, 10.2
Mnemonic: catch phrase or rhyme to aid memory 9.1
Molecule: group of atoms linked together 5.2, 5.4
Mordant: substance used to fix dye 9.2
Movement energy: energy in the form of movement (this makes appliances work) 1.3
Multicultural: many cultures 7.3
Muscle control: ability to control movement of fingers, hands, etc. 6.1

NSPCC: National Society for the Prevention of Cruelty to Children 2.4
National Marriage Guidance Council: organization which gives help to families 2.4
Natural causes: in the natural way of things 3.1
Night-cap: a bed-time drink, e.g. hot chocolate 1.3
Nightmare: frightening dream 6.2
Noise level: intensity of noise 4.4
Non combustible: does not catch fire 8.1
Non fiction: not imagined or invented 3.3
Notions: extra things needed to make an article, e.g. needles, pins, thread, buttons 10.3

Oesophagus: gullet 5.4
Order of priority: order with most important things first 1.1
Organization: group of people with a common purpose 2.3
Organize: plan; put together 1.2

PDSA: People's Dispensary for Sick Animals 2.4
Papilla: small bump on the tongue 5.3
Penetrate: get into 3.2, 9.3
Perishable food: food which spoils or decays 5.1
Personal hygiene: one's own cleanliness 4.2
Personality: person's individual qualities 6.2, 8.3
Physical growth: growth of the body 2.2
Physical properties: properties that can be seen or felt 7.3
Pictogram: a method of giving information using pictures or symbols 3.1
Piped water: water carried into premises through pipes 4.1
Planned buying: buying after careful thought 10.4
Point of sale: where items are paid for 10.2
Politician: person who takes an active part in the government of the country 3.1
Pollutant: something which causes impurities 4.4
Pollute: make dirty 4.1, 4.4
Pollution: spoiling of environment by man-made waste 4.4
Poor conductor: poor carrier (of electricity) 5.2
Potential: possible 6.3
Porous: allowing the passage of liquid or gas 4.1
Presser foot: part of the sewing machine which holds the fabric steady 7.4
Primary colour: cannot be made by mixing other colours 9.1
Printing: process of putting colour or pattern on fabric 9.3
Promotional leaflet: leaflet containing information to advertise a product 10.1
Public health inspector: person who checks on standards of hygiene in public places 4.2

RSPCA: Royal Society for the Prevention of Cruelty to Animals 2.4
Radiant: gives off heat and light when hot 7.1, 7.2

Radiation: transfer of heat energy by rays 5.2
Rancid: stale 5.3
Raw sewage: untreated human waste 4.1
Reassure: restore confidence 6.2
Recall: remember 3.1
Reference book: book in which you look for specialized information 3.3
Regional water authority: water authority responsible for a particular region 4.1
Regular: usual 1.1
Religious: concerning one's spiritual beliefs 2.3
Reputable: having a good reputation 4.3
Reputation: what people think about the character or qualities of someone 5.3
Research: to seek facts and information 3.3
Reservoir: place to store water 4.1
Resources: reserves of goods and money 1.1
Retail outlets: shops of all types 10.3
Returnable: can be taken back 10.2
Rotation of stock: using oldest items first 4.3
Routine: usual way of doing something 1.2
Royal purple: dye from a Mediterranean whelk 9.2
Run (dye): come out 9.2

Safe house: refuge 6.4
Saffron: dye made from dried orange-coloured stigmas of a type of crocus 9.2
Safety training: education for safety 3.4
Saliva: fluid in the mouth; more is secreted at the start of digestion of food 5.4
Sealed disc: solid plate in which the heating element is sealed in an electric hob 7.1
Secondary colour: colour made by mixing two primary colours 9.1
Segment: part of a circle 3.1
Select: choose 3.2
Selector: person who chooses 2.2
Self-centred: selfish 6.1
Self-locking: locking automatically 6.3
Sell-by date: date by which an item should be sold 4.3
Sense organ: part of the body which gathers information from outside the body 5.3
Sensitivity: ability to detect the feelings of others 2.2
Sensor: detector 7.1
Shelf-life: length of time something can be stored 4.3
Shopping precinct: enclosed area containing shops 3.4
Short-time work: work that is less than a normal working week 1.1
Skill: movement or action made easy by practice 1.1
Snack: refreshment or light meal 1.1
Social contact: mixing with other people 2.3
Social development: learning to relate to others 2.2
Social services: organization which aims to improve social conditions 2.4
Social skill: ability to relate to others 6.1
Society: group with a common interest 2.3
Solar energy: energy from the Sun 2.3
Statistics: information often in number form 6.3

Stimulate: rouse into action 5.3, 5.4, 6.1, 8.3
Stress: pressure and worry 4.4
Suffocation: death from lack of oxygen 6.3
Supermarket: large, self-service shop selling food and other goods 4.3
Surplus: more than is needed 10.4
Suspicion: feeling that something is likely 6.4
Swing needle: needle which can move from side to side 7.4
Symbol: representation of something 1.2, 3.1, 10.4

Taste bud: sense organ on the tongue 5.3
Team work: working together in a small group 2.2
Technology: applied scientific knowledge 3.2
Telephone directory: list of subscribers in alphabetical order 3.3
Temper tantrum: bout of violent temper 6.2
Template: pattern 8.3
Therm: unit of energy 1.4
Thermostat: device to control temperature 1.4
Tie-dyeing: method of creating patterns on cloth by tying it before dyeing 9.3
Time-plan: step by step order of work 1.2
Token: symbol 10.4
Tolerance: ability to put up with 5.3
Toxin: poison 5.1
Trademark: mark used by manufacturer to identify and distinguish his product 10.4
Treatment works: place where water is made safe 4.1
Trend: fashion 9.1
Trust: faith in another person 2.1
Tyrian purple: dye made from a Mediterranean whelk 9.2

Underestimate: estimate too low a value for something 6.3
Unit of electricity: a small set amount of electricity 1.4
Unstable: not balanced 6.3

Vacuum cleaner: a device for sucking up dirt 1.3
Vantage point: position giving a wide or clear view 3.4
Vet (veterinary surgeon): person qualified for the medical treatment of animals 1.2
Verbal directions: spoken directions 3.2
Vermin: unwanted animals that cause disease, e.g. mice, rats, lice, cockroaches, flies 4.3
Vibration: shaking or throbbing 5.2
Volume: amount of space taken up 1.4
Voluntary organization: group who give their services without pay 2.4

Wadding: padding 9.4
Water rate: charge made for using water 4.1
Water vapour: water in the form of a gas 4.1
Wattage: amount of electrical power 1.4
Welfare: well-being 2.4
White light: sunlight (made up of all the seven colours of the spectrum) 9.1
Woad: blue dye from the woad plant 9.2

Zig-zag stitch: stitch produced by a swing needle sewing machine 7.4